PLANTS AND IDEAS FOR YOUR GARDEN

PLANTS AND IDEAS FOR YOUR GARDEN

TIM SMITH

First published in 2009 by:

Grey-Mogg Books

ISBN: 978-0-9542588-1-8

Printed and bound in England by:

Forsyth & Steele
www.forsythandsteele.com

Cover images by Tim Smith

To my Mother who sowed seeds of annual flowers with me.
Which grew into a perennial enthusiasm for gardening.

HELLO AND WELCOME TO 'PLANTS AND IDEAS FOR YOUR GARDEN'...

The purpose of this book is to coach you in making, looking after and enjoying your garden. The chapters are a step-by-step explanation of how to turn a piece of ground into a garden. Answers to What?, Why?, How? and When?. The ideal first read for anyone who has never been into gardening. And for gardeners who can never get enough of plants and ideas for their garden!

CHAPTER ONE
'THE STATE OF NATURE'

Whatever state it is in the garden area surrounding your home is a world of interaction between soil, plants and insects. The only difference between a piece of ground left to its own devices and a garden is the type of plants growing there. Basically wild or civilised. Both have the same aim: reproduce themselves to secure their species survival. To achieve this the plants make flowers carrying a sugary substance called nectar along with pollen containing proteins, fats, sugar, vitamins and minerals. Foodstuffs essential for the existence of insects like bees, butterflies and moths. The lovely colours and scents associated with flowers are the plant's way of grabbing the insect's attention.

All because pollen is from the male part of the flower and contains the germ cell which needs to be introduced to its female counterpart to sexually reproduce the plant. This comes about through an insect entering a flower for food. Pollen is picked up on its body and on visiting another flower is brushed on to the female part; technically stigma and ovary connected by a style. The stigma receives the pollen which absorbs a sugary substance resulting in pollen tubes growing down through the style; carrying the male germ cell into one of several ovules within the ovary. It can now fuse with the female germ cell to form an embryo which will develop into a SEED. The ovary will grow into a FRUIT to enclose and protect the seeds.

Every seed is a flowering plant in limbo awaiting the cue to start growing. Known as GERMINATION this requires the right TEMPERATURE along with AIR and MOISTURE. The seed absorbs moisture causing it to swell splitting the outer seed coat. Moisture and oxygen now enter enabling the seed to breathe and draw on its stored food. The first root then emerges to anchor the seedling and starts to draw up moisture and nutrients from the soil. Next comes the shoot containing the growing tip. Finally the first leaves open enabling the seedling to feed by the process called photosynthesis. The green pigment in leaves; chlorophyll, absorbs light and uses it to make energy giving sugars from carbon dioxide and moisture in the air. These go down the stem to feed the developing roots which locate moisture and nutrients in the soil. For pumping back up the stem to fuel the plant's growth and development.

Both wild and civilised plants fall into two main categories.

‘ANNUALS’ and ‘PERENNIALS’. An annual will grow from seed, flower, set seed and die within the year. A perennial though will survive winter as a dormant crown either just below or above the soil surface. The season’s growth having flowered, set seed and withered. New growth will be triggered by an increase in temperature and light level. A third category ‘BIENNIALS’ refers to plants that take two years to grow from seed, flower, set seed and die. During their first season they make plenty of leaves to feed and produce a good root system. After winter dormancy they will develop their flowers and seeds.

Not all seeds fall on to the ground around the plant they have come from. Some are attached to a fluffy substance which catches the wind enabling the seed to be carried to a new spot. Insects such as ants move seeds around when nest-building. Other seeds have little hooks to hitch a lift on clothing or animal’s fur. Birds and animals eat fruit containing seeds which return to the ground in droppings and spewings. And there are seeds which are fired well away from the plant when their pods are ruffled.

There are six things which make up the structure of soil. Over millions of years water, wind, frost and heat have worn away local ROCK to a crumb-like texture. Mixed in with this is ORGANIC MATERIAL. The term for all the remains of plants and creatures that have died along with matter excreted by living creatures. This is pulled below ground by EARTHWORMS where it is broken down by MICROORGANISMS such as bacteria and fungi. By burrowing through the soil earthworms introduce AIR and their tunnels improve the drainage of WATER. Rainwater contains minerals which soak into the soil. Earthworms in feeding on organic matter also take in soil excreting undigested mineral matter at a level where plant roots feed. Other soil insects such as woodlice and beetles contribute to organic material by feeding on remains. In the creation of organic material chemical changes take place resulting in foods essential for plant development. Known as NUTRIENTS they are NITROGEN for LEAVES, PHOSPHATE for ROOTS and POTASH for FLOWERS.

Soil texture and its workability is determined by the size of its rock crumbs. The smaller they are the greater the water retention. Clay crumbs being the main example. When mixed with other minerals such as stones, sand or silt (from river valleys) it forms granules containing water, nutrients and organic matter. With air spaces in between it is ideal for plant roots to penetrate. Clay becomes a problem when these other minerals are scarce and the crumbs stick together. At the extreme they can form a solid layer, often waterlogged and hopeless for root development. But intermediately clay is very fertile retaining a high level of soluble plant nutrients. Its restricted aeration means that remains are processed more slowly so instead of organic material a substance called humus occurs. Dark, spongy and sticky it has the ability to slowly release nutrients to plants. The largest rock crumbs are sand which cannot stick together so giving free drainage. This type of soil warms quickly in spring encouraging early growth. However it soon dries out and the abundance of air causes bacterial oxidisation of the organic material. Some soil is very stony; often shallow containing unweathered local rock. In areas of chalk or limestone bedrock the soil will be characteristically white and stony yet fairly fertile.

CHAPTER TWO
'THE REFINEMENT OF NATURE'

Gardening is probably best described as the introduction of law and order to a piece of ground. The natural system is amazingly effective and so forms the basis for all gardening techniques. A good gardener will work within this system using their skills to enhance the power of nature.

Making a garden out of a wild piece of ground requires the gardener to show understanding, skill, sensitivity and judgement. But establishing horticultural civilisation is a revolution and upheaval is inevitable. Firstly wild plants have to make way for civilised plants. As soon as the decision is made to create a garden they are referred to as weeds. Secondly living creatures whose natural habits spoil refinement become known as pests.

Weeding is war and weeds never give up trying to reproduce themselves. Their weapons are seeds and roots. Your arsenal includes FORK, SPADE, HOE, HANDFORK and TROWEL. A chemical called GLYPHOSPHATE may also be needed.

ANNEX: 'TOOL UP!'

The best tools are marked 'tempered', 'heat-treated', 'forged' or 'drop-forged', made of stainless or carbon steel with shafts of ash wood. Kept clean and dry, shafts rubbed occasionally with linseed oil and blades with an oily rag they will rarely need replacing. Goldilocks tried the chairs, porridge and beds of the three bears before deciding which was 'just right' so handle several tools to ensure you get the most comfortable.

Basically there are two types of FORK - GARDEN FORK and a scaled-down lighter BORDER FORK. This is worth considering for lighter soils, smaller gardens or gardeners who are not Mr or Ms Muscle. SPADES are termed GARDEN and BORDER too. A good HOE to choose is the DUTCH HOE. A HANDFORK is a fork decreased in size for use one-handed and a TROWEL the spade equivalent. GLYPHOSPHATE is a chemical which kills weeds without leaving a damaging residue in the soil. It 'biodegrades' meaning that it is broken down by the soil microorganisms.

It would be helpful if you have known your chosen area for a while. A year would be ideal, especially if the ground has already been a garden. You would then be aware of any civilised plants that are worth saving and the sort of weedlife you are up against. The best time to make a move is when the weeds start growing so you can pinpoint your attack. Call on your fork; this can penetrate the hardest of ground; breaking it up into crumbly clods allowing the removal of deep rooted weeds. Put your foot down on the step of the fork to push it into the ground pulling back on the handle to break and loosen the soil. Lift the clod on the fork; turn it over removing weeds and checking no pieces of perennial root remain (if they do they will regrow). Also get rid of any builder's detritus or large stones which will inhibit growth. Now work the soil to a crumbly consistency with the fork. Work across the plot in a line from left to right starting the next row directly behind where you began. This is HARD WORK so do not do too much in one go and regret it afterwards! Over the next couple of months or so keep an eye open for any regrowth of perennial weeds and remove them. If the soil is particularly heavy then applying glyphosphate as directed may be an easier and more successful plan of campaign. The soil will contain a vast number of seeds from annual weeds which will constantly start germinating. Push and pull your hoe underneath these weedlings to uproot them on a warm day so they wither on the surface.

This close encounter with the soil will indicate its texture and workability, also whether it will need any improvement. Really heavy soil will benefit from a technique called 'double digging' so sharp gravel can be added to open it up and improve drainage. Double digging is probably the hardest job you will come across in gardening but the good news is that it is generally a once only task. A job for your spade it entails digging a trench to the depth of two spade blades across the plot. Into this goes the sharp gravel (from a builders merchant) which can be worked in thoroughly with the fork. While you are there include some organic material such as well rotted farmyard manure (at least a year old), spent mushroom compost or compost from your local authority. This will help to lighten the soil and encourage plant roots to grow down towards it where they will also find moisture. It is important to recognise 'topsoil' and 'subsoil'. Topsoil is where all the earthworms and microorganisms work on the organic material and contains the resulting plant nutrients. It can vary in depth. Underneath is the subsoil which is lighter in colour. Be careful not to mix them as this will destroy the working environment and goodness of the topsoil.

After indigenous weedlife has been blitzed and any soil

improvements carried out the soil should be disturbed as little as possible. This will conserve moisture and allow the soil dwellers to return to their peaceful existence processing organic material for the good of soil structure and fertility. Organic material is best introduced on to the surface of the soil in a layer 10cm (4") thick. Known as a MULCH this will lessen the evaporation of moisture from the soil surface and stop light reaching any annual weed seeds thwarting germination. In time it will be pulled into the soil by earthworms leading to improved drainage, moisture retention and fertility. This will be an ideal place for your plants to grow. If they have everything they need in water, light and nutrients then they are unlikely to become stressed. And stress-free plants are healthy plants much less susceptible to picking up disease.

Do not be tempted to over feed the soil with additional fertilisers. This can lead to plants making 'soft growth' which means their cells have thin walls leaving them more vulnerable to attack from disease and pests. If a particular plant is known to benefit from added enrichment or the soil is distinctly unfit then it may be a good idea to resort to fertilisers. Use organic fertilisers - those which are derived from living creatures such as 'BLOOD, FISH AND BONE' and ones which include natural minerals like SEAWEED. (Wear GARDENING GLOVES when handling fertilisers). These will filter into the soil joining the rest of the organic material to be worked on by the microorganisms creating extra nutrients.

It is interesting to find out if your soil is 'acid' or 'alkaline'. There are more than enough wonderful plants that will make a lovely garden whatever the verdict. However one way or the other could influence plant selection and garden layout or alert you to some corrective action. You will need to buy a SOIL TESTING KIT. Take several samples from different parts of the garden testing them individually. The process involves putting a little bit of dry soil into a test tube adding some of the supplied indicator dye. Follow the instructions and then compare the resulting colour shades with the chart. Acidity and alkalinity are measured on a scale called pH. Soils range from pH 4 to 8.5; 7 being neutral, 4 extremely acid and 8.5 extremely alkaline. For most plants a level of 6.0 to 6.5 is very acceptable. If you get a low pH reading and therefore have an acid soil spent mushroom compost which contains lime or straight GARDEN LIME will help to reduce acidity. Acid soils are likely to be short of magnesium and calcium; important nutrients so DOLOMITE or MAGNESIAN LIMESTONE will redress the balance.

CHAPTER THREE
'LOOK AND LEARN'

Knowing your garden-to-be over a year is useful because you become aware of which parts are dry or moist, where and when sunlight, shade and moonlight occur and how the wind prevails. This time can also be well spent simply learning from looking.

Looking at other peoples efforts. Buy 'The Yellow Book' - produced yearly by The National Gardens Scheme and available in bookshops from February/March. 'A county by county guide to thousands of gardens of quality, character and interest'. Opened to raise money for charity there is no more pleasant way to get ideas for garden design and plant association; along with tips on practical grow-how from the gardeners themselves. Talking to garden owners (often over a nice cup of tea and cracking cake) is frequently a confidence booster too as many will admit to having little or no experience when starting their garden. Look out for advertisements for other garden openings.

When you are enjoying a garden cast your minds eye back to your own ground to see if what you like could be created there. Basically most plant associations and a lot of features can be replicated simply by scaling up or down according to the space available. The majority of plants you will come across are both affordable and easily available. Take some photographs and jot down names of plants and combinations you like for reference. Note if the situation is dry or moist, light or shade. However the greatest impact a garden can have on a visitor is to kick-start their very own creative thought. And there is absolutely no reason to doubt your ability to come up with unique and innovative design and plant associations. Everything that is now accepted as classic was once an individual's very own creative thought.

Many more gardens can be 'visited' through magazines and newspapers. Here you can draw on ideas and information from celebrated gardeners. Enjoy the pictures but bear in mind that photographic technique is capable of enhancement! Television gardening programmes are useful in showing professional gardeners handling tools and the 'what?, when?, how? and why?' of routine jobs through the year. Look around where you live and especially at your house seeing which types of brick, stone and style predominate. Consider how these can be used in the construction of walls and paths to blend your garden into its surroundings. Try and talk to local gardeners to learn from their experiences of growing in the area.

ANNEX : 'TOOL UP!'

It is time to get a HOSE. Ultimately for watering but firstly for shaping your flower borders. Select a hose long enough to reach the furthest point of your garden-to-be. Bear in mind that in time this will be via a rather indirect route to avoid damaging plants and features! A good hose is one made of 5-ply vinyl-nylon. It should come with a nozzle which can be twisted to deliver water on a scale from gentle spray to monsoon. If your house does not have an OUTSIDE WATER TAP arrange for one to be fitted for convenient watering.

CHAPTER FOUR
'TIME FOR DESIGN':- 'THE BOUNDARY LINE'

Physically defining the extremities of your ground is essential to mark what is legally yours and to provide security, shelter and an attractive background for plants. Achieved through walls, fences and hedges. Which you choose depends on where your garden-to-be is situated, personal preference and how much you can afford to spend.

What lies beyond your site is a major consideration. Basically if it is pleasing to look at - trees, attractive architecture, rolling countryside then it would be nice to use this as a backdrop for your garden and not block it out with a dominant boundary. However if you are faced with an unlovely industrial or urban picture then hiding it as much as possible would be an advantage.

How the wind prevails also needs to be thought about. Wind cannot filter through walls, fences and evergreen hedges so gets forced up, over and down into the garden (roughly at a spot 2x the height of the boundary from the boundary) causing buffeting and wind-chill. Experience is showing that climate evolution is giving rise to volatile weather and outside of the traditional seasonal boxes. The possibility of very strong winds needs to be taken into account when deciding on a boundary. To get an idea of what a fence has to contend with I suggest two of you visit a garden centre during a gale and both get hold of a fence panel while standing in an exposed area! The conclusion being that although a fence is an attractive reasonably low-cost option; its future durability is questionable. Especially if your site is prone to wind. Basically go to a top-class tradesman who can construct a fence from the best materials, over-engineered both in design and erection for the greatest chance of a long and useful life. The natural beauty of wood will be enhanced and longevity increased through regular applications of a quality preservative - the oilier the better to repel moisture.

A large number of our stately homes have a 'walled garden'. Enclosing a garden behind a wall was particularly popular with the Victorians; not just for shelter but as an opportunity to grow plants vertically. The ability of a wall to retain warmth and to radiate between a ¼ and 1 degree of heat by night was another plus. The fact that many of these walls have lasted for well over a century proves that with good materials and construction durability is assured. Obviously a wall is the most expensive of the boundary options but requires the least maintenance. If it can match the style, brick or stone used for your house then it has the added value of uniting home and garden. Especially if the same material can be used for paths and hard surfaces throughout the garden. If your garden is in undulating countryside then a wall or fence with a wavy top would be complimentary. A reclamation yard is worth visiting - not for cheapness but in the interests of recycling and combining the new and existing as seamlessly as possible.

Both walls and fences are relatively quick to construct with instant impact on the garden in terms of view, privacy, wind behaviour, shadow and soil moisture within their lee. Conversely hedge material can be selected from a vast list of potential cultivars. Planting although straightforward is followed by regular training and tending for evermore. There can be no vertical planting as with a fence and wall, indeed space needs to be left to access maintenance. Significantly there will be several years while the hedge establishes during which your site will lack the protection a developing garden appreciates. It also has to thrive and that cannot be guaranteed even with the best attention. However the hedge is the only LIVING boundary although they are all naturalistic - fences generally from wood and walls made of materials from the ground - stone and brick (from clay). Uniquely a hedge will provide shelter and food for birds. Its height can be tailored to either screen or accentuate.

Deciding on a hedge generates the question of 'evergreen or deciduous?'. Evergreen in the form of conifers is tempting; on average faster growing without the drawback of being 'see-through' in winter. However, many people rue the day that they or a neighbour chose Cupressocyparis 'leylandii' for a hedge. Although not fair to judge all conifers by leylandii's behaviour the moral of the story is to allow a conifer hedge to grow to the desired height and then cut the leading growth 15cm (6") below. Followed by a light trimming of the sides. An all over trim must be carried out in spring, midsummer and late summer so that a dense even surface is created. If this is overlooked the hedge will grow higher and wider than is practical with re-shaping impossible as conifers cannot produce new shoots from old wood. In coastal areas conifers can suffer irretrievable die-back from salty winds. In frosty weather spray conifers with water to replace moisture lost through the needles during the cold.

TIM'S CHOICE:-

THUJA PLICATA ATROVIRENS (Western Red Cedar)

A quick growing conifer ideal for making a neat, dense hedge. The foliage withstands the necessary trimming and gives off an attractive aroma. If you include a traditional wooden greenhouse in your garden it will quite likely be made of Western Red Cedar which will be complimentary. Plant 45cm (18") apart.

There are plenty of evergreens other than conifers. Both evergreen and deciduous hedging plants need to be reduced by half following planting. The exceptions are those whose natural inclination is to form a trunk such as Beech which can be cut back by ⅓. In the following year's midsummer soft shoot tips can be pinched out and longer leading shoots cut back by no more than ⅓. In winter further reduce the plants by ⅓. In successive years simply trim into the required shape. But with Beech leave alone during the winter until a year later when they can be reduced by ⅓. Then trimming to shape can begin the following year; preferably in cool wet weather to conserve moisture. This cutting back in the hedge's formative years encourages thick bushy growth which is the mark of a good impenetrable hedge.

Technically in an unpruned shoot the main bud produces a hormone which inhibits the growth of the secondary buds behind it. If the main bud is removed along with its hormone then the secondary buds will grow more strongly. Harder pruning will stimulate remaining buds into vigorous growth leading to a bushy habit.

Before planting any hedge erect a temporary wind breaking screen of mesh (available from garden centres) along the actual boundary as a marker and protector. Prepare the soil as outlined in Chapter Two. Mark the planting line which should be as far out from the temporary screen to allow the hedge to develop to the required width.

A nursery specialising in hedging is the best place to buy but many garden centres have a good range too. Most will be pot grown and it is advisable to select plants that do not look as if they have been hanging around a long while and are pot-bound. Smaller plants will often get away quicker than larger ones as well as being cheaper to buy and easier to handle. Check that the plant looks healthy and undamaged in root, stem and growth accumulating plants of the same height and proportion. An ideal time to buy would be autumn/early winter or early spring when the soil is moist and either still warm or warming to encourage root activity. Do make sure that the species on sale have been propagated from British stock because if not a flowering hedge may try and perform at a time at odds with our seasons.

Before planting make sure that the plants have had a thorough soaking the previous 24 hours. Dig each hole with your spade and remove the plants from their pots teasing out the soil from between the roots. Adjust the roots which have grown the circular way of the pot arranging them in the hole so they will strike out into the surrounding soil. Backfill with soil and FIRM well with your boot. A mulch of organic matter will help conserve moisture and warmth. The new hedge MUST be kept watered with your hose and weed free. An annual organic mulch and a sprinkling of an organic fertiliser such as Blood Fish and Bone in springtime will encourage healthy growth.

TIM'S CHOICE:-

BEECH - FAGUS SYLVATICA. My favourite! Because although deciduous it retains its coppery dead leaves during winter providing screening and shelter. Along with a lovely glow in winter light and a delightful rustle. Leaf retention is encouraged by regular trimming. Wonderful fresh green foliage in spring. Copes with shallow soil and exposure but not extremely wet conditions. Only drawback is a somewhat sedate growth rate and susceptability to beech aphid. As an alternative to the green try PURPUREA, the slower growing purple-leaved form. Space 30cm (1') apart.

HAWTHORN (QUICKTHORN) - CRATAEGUS MONOGYNA. Also known as May this deciduous hedge has numerous thorns and glossy leaves dark green on the top and paler underneath. Fragrant white flowers with pink anthers (they contain the pollen within the stamens; the male fertilising organ) in late spring. Not as its name suggests quick off the mark but when established growth rate will increase especially on lighter soil. Diligent pruning will create a good, dense hedge. Trim in early spring and in late summer. A haven for insects and nesting birds. Space 30cm (1') apart.

ANNEX: 'TOOL UP!'

If you do decide on a hedge then now is the time to buy some tools to carry out the pruning and trimming. Firstly a HAND PRUNER often known as SECATEURS. Ultimately you will use these virtually every time you are gardening. For removing dead flowers and growth and for shaping hedges, shrubs and trees. This justifies getting the very best that you can afford. If you can run to Swiss made FELCO pruners then they could well last you for life as replacement blades and other parts are available. Recommended are 'Felco 7 Professional' which will tackle branches up to 25mm (1") which should be the capability of any quality make you choose. Always check that your pruners feel comfortable in your hand.

For trimming your hedge a pair of HEDGE SHEARS will be needed. Again go for the best with ash handles to absorb the shock of the cutting action from your hands and either stainless-steel or forged carbon steel for the blades.

A handy little gadget is a CERAMIC FILE - a pocket-sized sharpening stone for keeping blades sharp while working.

POINT OF ORDER!: ALWAYS clean soil off tool blades when you have finished with them. Store them in a secure place out of sight and the weather. Occasionally wipe blades with a rag soaked in engine oil to keep them bright and corrosion free. Squirt a little oil on to the pivots of pruners to maintain condition and performance. In winter arrange for any cutting tools that have lost their edge to be sharpened professionally. Be careful on their return! Wooden shafts will appreciate being rubbed with a rag soaked in linseed oil from time to time. Check that all nuts and screws are secure tightening loose ones or replacing any that are missing.

The pruning and training of the plants that will eventually make up your garden is an intricate business which can be made considerably easier with an illustrated guide. So you can confidentally go about the job and get the very best out of your plants I would suggest that you buy a book dedicated to the subject. There are several good ones but the 'ROYAL HORTICULTURAL SOCIETY PRUNING AND TRAINING' by Christopher Brickell and David Joyce is definitive covering over 800 trees, shrubs, roses and climbers. There is detailed infomation on general pruning principles and the growth habits and particular needs of individual plants.

CHAPTER FIVE
'TIME FOR DESIGN':- 'SHAPING BORDERS, MAKING PATHS, LAYING GRASS'

Now your boundary is sorted out you can turn your attention to working out the form of the main physical features. This is approached through using shape and perhaps surprisingly; illusion. If your garden area is oblong then the longest dimension is the diagonal so basing a border on this will suggest it is bigger than it actually is. Curves and zig-zags make a short distance appear longer as you catch sight of things at a slower pace. Circular borders give an impression of width and space. Using the diagonal for a path will give borders greater depth and thus more room for plants. In a compact area constructing paths from small units of paving such as bricks or tiles will make the space appear larger. Tapering the path towards its end also makes the distance look further. The smaller garden requires the utmost of creative thought to ensure every square metre makes an imaginative contribution to the whole.

Borders designed around the diagonal are known as 'islands'. Having walk-round access makes maintenance considerably easier. Plants can also be seen more closely and from every angle. Island borders need to have bold sweeping informal curves. Look at an atlas for some ideas using your hose to map out shapes on the ground. If you have an upstairs or some other safe elevated position make use of it for added perspective. As an alternative a border could sweep in and out from the side boundaries to disguise the shape of the garden area. This could be seen as the 'mainland'; 'offshore' around the middle of the area an island border (or borders) could be constructed to appear as if it or they had broken away from the 'mainland'.

Raised borders are a consideration for those who find bending difficult or garden from a wheelchair. Basically they are walled planters so will need constructing at the same time as any boundary wall. Mortar will need to be left out of a verticle joint every 90cm (3') for drainage and the inside waterproofed. The borders can then be filled with an appropriate soil mixture, the added height providing an opportunity to enjoy plants nearer eye-level and at close quarters.

Hard surfaces are a necessity in gardens. To give clean and easy access to house, shed, greenhouse, wheelie bins etc. There are many materials available subject to affordability. If using brick, especially reclaimed do make sure it is hard enough to be frostproof - engineering bricks are ideal especially the dark grey ones which accentuate green. If you can find reclaimed bricks bearing a local name this will add some historical interest to your garden. Remember to choose materials which are attractive but not dominant and are in keeping with your house and surroundings. So that the essential paving blends into the garden extend it out as an edge to the borders. For a firm maintenance-free definition plus a hard-standing from which work can be carried out and the plants admired. Seemingly contradictorily it will also soften the edge by giving plants somewhere where they can naturally encroach without causing problems. The paving can then be continued out to a central feature in the garden thus linking everything together.

To further meld paving into the garden gaps of different sizes can be left between the bricks, stones or whatever so that plants can be incorporated. This reduces the formal impact by making the paving into a living part of the garden while preserving practicality. Gravel is an effective material for simultaneously complimenting and relieving paving. Coming in many different colours and textures (which can also be effectively mixed together) it fuses naturally with the hue and appearance of the mixed border. Gravel is best laid 5-10cm (2-4") deep on top of a liner available from garden centres. You could even consider using coal. Especially if mining was a local feature to give your garden a historical tie. Mainly though because it contrasts brilliantly with variegated foliage and white, yellow, red and orange flowers. Slate too comes in neutral colours which can link house and garden while inviting a wide spectrum of both complimentary and contrasting colours from your planting.

The area remaining after borders and paving have taken shape may be the final pre-planting stage in the garden but just as important because it is the foreground for your borders. Laying grass is traditional and for one very good reason. It is GREEN. Soothing, restful and recessive enhancing other colours through contrast. The colour of nature herself a grass area is a perfect place to sit or stand and enjoy what the garden is giving.

ANNEX: 'TOOL UP'

Before starting on your grass you will need to get a FLATHEAD STEEL RAKE. The best are forged from carbon steel with ash handles. A really useful tool for combing together stones, breaking down soil into fine particles and levelling it prior to sowing seeds or laying turf. Another good purchase would be a WIZARD RAKE which has short stiff rubber tines for combing leaves and debris from grass. Buy a good quality stiff BROOM to keep your paved areas tidy.

The HALF-MOON EDGER is worth getting to initially cut turves to shape but mainly to remove grass when it grows over paving. Go for one with a stainless-steel or carbon steel blade. Push your foot down on to the steel step above the blade to make a clean cut where the grass meets the paving.

Now you are engaging in serious shifting of materials and plants around the garden a WHEELBARROW is essential. Go for one that feels comfortable to handle; can be manoeuvred easily within the confines of your garden and suits the work you want it to do. An ideal wheelbarrow has a pneumatic tyre which makes for an easier, smoother and more stable push. Also it will not leave a damaging track. A tipper bar in front of the wheel will give stability when tipping. The strongest wheelbarrows have a reinforced frame with either a galvanised or baked epoxy finish for the pan. Longevity can be increased with an occasional coat of paint and a squirt of oil to the axle. A nicely painted wheelbarrow is as traditional to a garden as a robin sitting on a spade!

And finally for the moment a LAWN MOWER. If your area of grass is reasonably compact and you are reasonably fit a HAND-PROPELLED MOWER is a sensible choice. Here is an opportunity to enjoy a brisk walk in your garden; lightly using your muscles while deeply breathing in fresh air permeated with the scent of flowers. No noise apart from a gentle whirr in keeping with the working bees. Not another demand on oil or electricity. A rare chance to work at your pace rather than that of a machine; the frenzy of which often leaves grass (and hedges) looking decidedly battle weary.

Do visit a dedicated lawnmower shop which not only sells mowers but advises and SERVICES as well. Try and find one with the expertise to restore classic models from Qualcast, Atco, Webb and Ramsomes to A1 condition. They will not be cheap but their durability is like London Routemaster buses. Kept clean and well-oiled with an occasional service they will serve you for a long time. An alternative way is to find one in a second-hand shop, on a tip or buck-shee from a gardener with other plans. Then take it to the shop for rejuvenation.

Hand-propelled mowers either have a wheel each side of the cutters or a cylinder roller immediately behind the blades. This is the best arrangement giving the traditional striped finish.The wheeled model is lighter, more manoeuvrable and especially suited to cutting banks or around trees. The greater number of blades give the finest cut.

Alternatively there is the hovermower where an electric motor creates a downdraft of air to move the machine while driving a single rotary blade. And more expensive both to buy and maintain are petrol aspirated rotaries and cylinder mowers powered by petrol, electricity or car battery. For longevity go for a motor with a capacity GREATER than is needed for its actual workload. Always read instruction booklets and heed routine maintenance and service advice. Be very careful of trailing cables and INSTALL A CIRCUIT- BREAKER to prevent electrocution if the cable is severed.

Basically the cutters on a hand-propelled mower are operating considerably slower than on powered mowers so the grass is less likely to be tugged or shaved. Cutters need to be set around 1cm (½"). Putting a machine on to wet grass will just flatten the grass and clog the cutters. Any cylinder or petrol rotary mower simply requires the gardener to walk in a line and then back again slightly overlapping on the previous stripe. With hovermowers the technique is more like vacuuming a carpet. These like petrol rotaries are ideal for banks and longer grass. If you use a hovermower once a week the very fine clippings produced will organically enrich the grass if left behind. However longer clippings would exclude light so are best collected in a grass-box attached to the mower.

Before making a grass area prepare the soil as in Chapter Two. Heavy soil will need some sharp sand or horticultural grit forking in. Then using your RAKE remove any stones or debris from the surface tamping the crumbly soil level with the back of the tool. Then compact it by shuffling forward with your feet close together. Apply an organic fertiliser such as Blood, Fish and Bone before raking north/south then east/west to the required level. When laying turves work from a thick broad plank to avoid compressing the soil or the laid grass. Work sifted soil into the gaps between the turves and make sure they butt together and against any paving.

Turf is the most expensive way to make a grass area but the easiest to lay with an instant effect. Make sure you buy quality hardwearing grass from a reputable supplier and not at a time when there is a possibility of prolonged dry weather or frost. Lay straightaway and keep checking that the area has a good moisture content especially during establishment. If using seed choose a hardwearing, drought resistant mix and sow evenly over the surface. Ideally this should take place March to May or August/ September. Again keep the soil moist while the grass establishes but be careful using a hose that you give an extremely gentle spray to avoid washing the seed and soil to peaks and troughs. Allow to grow to 7cm (3") then set your mower blades high and give the first cut. A hand-propelled mower is ideal as it will roll the grass as well as giving a gentle cut. Lower the blades for subsequent cuts.

CHAPTER SIX
'TREES - USING, CHOOSING AND PLANTING'

When you start introducing plants to your area of prepared soil it is a great moment. The point at which you can proudly claim to have a GARDEN! In residential areas trees are second in conspicuousness to buildings. That makes them ideal for reducing the dominance of buildings giving both shelter and privacy. Trees reduce wind chill in a garden, create shadow, form an attractive backdrop for plantings and provide food and shelter for birds. They can also frame and therefore accentuate features both within and beyond the garden for added impact. And be focal points individually or grouped in odd numbers within borders and grass areas.

There are several points to bear in mind when considering trees for a garden. The long-term view must be taken to envisage the tree when it approaches maturity. Its height, spread and shape should be in scale with your house and garden. How the tree develops below ground is important too with regard to drains, inspection covers and building foundations. The shape and colour of the foliage is for aesthetic contemplation but think if the density of the leaves will rob the house and garden of valuable light. Consider what conditions are conducive to the tree's wellbeing and if your garden and area has them. See which trees tick the boxes in respect of attractive bark, interesting branching and seasonal noteworthiness such as flower, scent, leaf colour and fruit.

Unfortunately the life of a tree is generally longer than that of the person who plants it so it pays to put in the very best from a dedicated tree specialist. If possible go for what are known as 'bare-rooted whips'. These are young trees that have been grown in a field and lifted for sale. Being smaller they are cheaper, easier to handle and will establish quickly. On the other hand a tree that has spent just enough time in a container to produce a nice fibrous root system is well placed to make a reasonably quick getaway. It is these fibrous roots that strike out for food within the soil and establish the top growth of the tree. The nursery could supply you with an 'inoculant of mycorrhizal fungi' which can be applied to the soil to encourage the development of these fine feeder roots.

The ideal time to be buying trees is autumn/early winter when the soil is warm and moist enough to stimulate root development. A deciduous tree is a perennial which survives winter by holding its dormant buds on a branching structure. Until an increase in temperature and light level ends their dormancy. When temperature and light level fall the tree's reserves of sugars produced by photosynthesis are diverted from top growth to root growth. As the chlorophyll breaks down other pigments in the leaves show through. Carotenoids become visible as the yellows and oranges of autumn while anthocyanins the reds and purples. If autumn has plenty of bright sunny days and some crisp cold nights sugars will accumulate in the leaves producing more anthocyanins. Never plant during frost, in waterlogged ground or in summer when copious watering would be needed to keep the tree alive.

Discard any tree that has damage to its trunk or limbs. Make sure the canopy is in proportion to the diameter of the trunk; if not it could snap in a strong wind. Grafted trees must have a sound union between trunk and rootstock. Check for healthy looking dormant buds and if the tree is in leaf or evergreen that the growth is lively. Try and inspect the root system for damage or debility from lack of moisture.

With your spade dig a hole three times either the diameter of the roots of a bare-rooted tree or the container that it was in. Remove the soil to a depth of 30cm (1'). Fork around EXCEPT where the tree will sit. This is to help drainage while avoiding the settlement of soil under the rootball. Which would cause the tree to be below the correct planting depth. Cut off any roots above where the main roots naturally emanate. This is called the 'root flare' which needs to be level with or slightly above the surrounding soil even if this was not so in a container. Tease out soil from between the roots arranging them so they can strike out into the surrounding soil. Especially important if they have begun growing the circular way of a container. Backfill with soil only (no extra organic matter); the roots must be encouraged to venture beyond the planting hole for nutrients to establish the tree. They will not do this if they can find what they need within the hole and anchorage will be compromised. In time as organic matter becomes part of the soil its bulk decreases with resulting settlement leaving the root flare too exposed. Firm gently with your heel working towards the tree from the outside of the hole. Trees in excess of 1.2m (4') must be staked. Drive a stake at 45 degrees over the rootball into the prevailing wind. Attach the stake 45-60cm (18-24") from the ground to the trunk with a well cushioned firm tie (available from garden centres). This ensures that the roots are well anchored but thc trunk can move with the wind stimulating good strong development. Keep the tree well watered especially during the first season and check the tie regularly; loosening it to keep pace with growth.

TIM'S CHOICE:-

BIRCH (BETULA) - Absolutely perfect! Birch have a graceful habit and quite quickly give a developing garden a light airy feel of maturity. The combination of fine form and small leaves softens the impact of buildings; creating flickering sylvan shadows without impairing light and view. From even the slightest breeze a delightful rustle ensues and in season catkins will shimmy. (Catkins are flowerheads composed of many individual blooms densely attached to a single stem. Pollen grains being released by wind for pollination). Crowns are narrow and upright showing off the attractive bark making birch ideal for the more compact garden. The coloured bark is especially attractive in winter when the entire structure of the tree can be admired. Birch are renowned for autumn leaf colour. Happy in moisture retentive well-drained soil in full sun but will tolerate light soil and exposed positions. Their surface roots will not undermine foundations. Grass cannot be suffocated by fallen leaves as their shape allows air to circulate between them; if gathered and spread on your borders they will quickly decompose. Little pruning is needed mainly to accentuate the shape and alluring bark. Never prune a birch when the sap is rising as the wounds can leak damaging amounts of sap. Birch are enchanting whether planted as isolated specimens or in groups of odd numbers.

SPECIES:-

B. ALBOSINENSIS variety SEPTENTRIONALIS - a slender tree with pale-red peeling bark with a greyish bloom. Oval mid-green leaves covered in short silky hairs turning yellow in autumn. 6cm (2½") long yellow-brown catkins open with the young leaves. 7.5m (25') high, 3m (10') across.

B. ALLEGHANIENSIS LUTEA - peeling yellow-brown bark and oval matt yellow-green leaves turning yellow in autumn. Aromatic shoots. Yellow-brown catkins 10cm (4") long in early spring. 9m (30') high, 4.5m (15') across.

B. ERMANII - cream-pink peeling bark and oval mid-green leaves turning yellow in autumn. Yellow-brown catkins 10cm (4") open with the young leaves. 9m (30') high, 4.5m (15') across.

B. UTILIS variety JACQUEMONTII - dazzling white peeling bark.

Tapered oval dark green leaves turning yellow in autumn. Yellow-brown catkins 12cm (5") long in early spring. When bark peels the tree is actually shedding its 'old skin' revealing the new spotless bark underneath giving contrast of colour and texture. Wonderful in moonlight. 7.5m (25') high, 4.5m (15') across.
variety JERMYNS has the same white bark but larger catkins 15cm (6") or more.
variety SILVER SHADOW - again with white bark but pendent dark green leaves.
variety GRAYSWOOD GHOST- white bark and very glossy leaves. 6m (20') high, 4.5m (15') across.

B. PENDULA (SILVER BIRCH) - the 'lady of the woods'; weeping branch tips and silvery peeling bark. Diamond-shaped toothed mid-green leaves turning yellow in autumn. 6cm (2½") long yellow-brown catkins in early spring. 9m (30') high, 3.5m (12') across.
variety LACINIATA or DALECARLICA - drooping branches and deeply cut leaves.
variety YOUNGII - dome-shaped weeping tree with delicate leaves. 4.5m (15') high, 2.2 m (7') across.

B. PAPYRIFERA - known as the paperbark birch this tree has thinly peeling bright white bark with a waxy bloom; the newly exposed bark being pale orange-brown. Oval dark green leaves turning yellow to orange in autumn. Yellow catkins 10cm (4") long in early spring. 9m (30') high, 4.5m (15') across.

To highlight birch's fabulous bark some dark evergreens can be considered:- JUNIPERUS COMMUNIS SENTINEL - handsome narrow and erect 1.5m (5') high, 60cm (2') across. Needle-like evergreen leaves. Appreciates well-drained soil in full sun or dappled shade.

ABIES KOREANA - conical fir bearing erect violet-blue cones (5-7cm 2-3" long) on shiny dark green branches glistening white underneath. In spring the tree has upright rows of pink, crimson or green flowers. 4.5m (15') high, 1.8m (6') across. Moist well-drained soil in full sun or dappled shade.

PINE (PINUS) variety FASTIGIATA - a slender upright Scots pine 8m (25') high, 1-3m (3-10') across. Ridged purple-grey bark at base becoming

flaky red-brown or orange towards the crown. Twisted blue-green leaves in pairs and oval cones 3-7cm (1¼-3") long ripening to grey or red-brown.
variety ARISTATA (Bristle cone pine) - 3m (10') high, 1.5m (5') across. Dense conical tree, grey-green leaves with flecks of white resin carried in bunches. Young needles have blue-white inner sides. Long oval brown cones 4-10cm (1½-4") long with a bristly prickle on each scale. Smooth dark grey bark and red-brown hairy shoots.

Pines appreciate a sunny position in well-drained soil. Pine needles will not freeze so can be gathered up and used to cover plants that are susceptible to frost damage. These trees are particularly attractive in winter light and especially if frost is present.

BEECH (FAGUS) - as beautiful a tree as when used as a hedge! Attractive smooth grey bark.
variety SYLVATICA AUREA PENDULA - a narrow tree with pendulous branches and bright yellow young foliage maturing to green. Best in light shade growing to 4.5m (15') high and 1.5m (5') across. Russet autumn tints.
variety SYLVATICA DAWYCK PURPLE - deep purple foliage and a narrow columnar habit. 9m (30') high, 2m (7') across. DAWYCK GOLD is especially narrow with bright yellow young foliage turning yellow-green in summer. RED OBELISK has purple wavy-edged leaves and produces a second flush of plum-red growth in July.

ACER GRISEUM (Paper-bark maple) - 4.5m (15') high, 2.5m (8') across but slow growing. Peeling/curling cinnamon-coloured bark revealing orange-brown patches. Toothed, three-lobed mid-green leaves turn a stunning orange/red in autumn. If you can, plant this tree so that the sun sets behind it giving the bark an aura of burnished copper. Likes a moisture retentive free-draining soil. Any pruning should be done in the dormant season to avoid sap leakage.

ACER PENSYLVANICUM (Snake-bark maple) - 6m (20') high, 3m (10') across. An upright tree with green and white striped bark. Bright green leaves are tinged pink when young and turn rich yellow in autumn.
variety ERYTHROCLADUM has brilliant pink shoots; striking in winter which become orange/red with white stripes as they mature.
ACER RUFINERVE differs in having leaves which turn red in autumn and red-winged fruit following greenish-yellow flowers held in erect clusters.

ACER PALMATUM SANGO-KAKU - vivid coral-pink shoots in winter. Deep 5-lobed leaves turn from orange/yellow to soft yellow in autumn. 4.5m (15') high, 2.5m (8') across.

PRUNUS SERRULA - 4.5m (15') high, 2.5m (8') across. Glistening, mahogany-like red/brown peeling bark which looks particularly effective when illuminated in the low light of a winter's morning or summer's evening. Dark green leaves turn yellow in autumn. Small white flowers in mid-spring develop into oval cherry-like fruit.

PRUNUS DULCIS ROSEOPLENA (Common almond) - 8m (25') high and across. Double pink flowers on bare shoots in spring followed by oval velvety-green fruit each containing an edible nut. (a 'double' flower has more petals than a 'single' with few if any stamens - the male reproductive part of the flower). Dark green leaves. Likes a moisture retentive free-draining soil in full sun.

CORYLUS AVELLANA CONTORTA (Corkscrew hazel) - noted for curiously twisted shoots and branches which are very effective in winter when they bear fuzzy yellow catkins. Mid-green leaves turning yellow in autumn. Requires well-drained soil in sun or dappled shade. Remove any straight shoots coming from the base of the tree and prune out branches that are crossing or tangling to preserve the unique appearance. Very slow growing.
variety PURPUREA has dark purple foliage, purple-tinged catkins and fruit husks. Grow this one in full sun.

SORBUS HUPEHENSIS (Hubei rowan) variety OBTUSA - 6m (20') high, 3.5m (12') across with ascending branches. Up to 15 oval blue/green leaflets on stems to 15cm (6") long, turning red in autumn. In late spring bears clusters of white flowers followed by spherical white berries (popular with Thrushes) which ripen to dark pink. Ideal conditions are organically enriched soil with good drainage in full sun or light dappled shade.

MALUS RED SENTINEL - this crab apple 4.5m (15') high, 3.5m (10') across has oval dark green leaves which follow white flowers in late spring. Fruit develop; firstly yellow flushed with red and then glossy dark red some 2.5cm (1") across. These remain on the bare branches throughout the winter until the blossom forms the following spring. Moist well-drained soil in sun or partial shade.

Obviously this choice is a fraction of the trees available to the gardener. However most gardens will not be able to accomodate many trees and these have been chosen for their size and interest throughout the year. 'Tim's Ten' is one more than Lancelot 'Capability' Brown (1715-1783); the celebrated designer of English landscaped gardens offered his clients! Do THINK CAREFULLY before you plant a tree to ensure it is suitable and in the right position. Once it has started to grow a tree will rarely thrive if subjected to replanting.

CHAPTER SEVEN
'SHRUBS - USING AND CHOOSING FOR WINTER INTO SPRING'

'Shrubs' sounds dull and uninteresting; in keeping with the hackneyed and hacked litter attractors around car-parks and public conveniences. But well chosen shrubs are a significant part of garden design being the next level of focus down from trees. The main difference is shrubs have several stems while trees grow from a single stem or trunk. Shrubs need to meet the same expectations as trees in terms of flower, scent, leaf colour, fruit and form. They too serve to screen, highlight features and plantings and be special attractions in their own right. Their prescence will influence conditions for the final level of planting (the mixed border) in terms of wind behaviour, light level and soil moisture. But it is the shrubs that perform during winter into spring that make the greatest impact blowing away the myth that this is a time devoid of colour and scent. Shrubs are the link to a 365 day garden of interest and require the same care choosing, buying and planting as trees.

TIM'S CHOICE:-

HAMAMELIS (Witch hazel) - has got everything; flowers appear to spark from bare branches accompanied by a zesty citrus-like perfume from mid-winter to early spring. Fantastic autumn leaf colour as well. In general varieties with orange to red flowers have leaves which turn orange, red and purple in autumn while those with yellow flowers show yellow tints. Slow growing to a height and spread of 1.8-3m (6-10'). Refrain from incorporating organic matter into the planting hole which should be in a place that gets sunshine in winter to enhance the flowers. On the other hand avoid a spot which becomes hot and dry in summer or the leaves will scorch. Mulching will help to prevent this. Very water retentive areas are not liked by these shrubs. Planting out of the wind will help to contain the scent and maximum benefit will be derived if this is near to your door, windows and path. Bear in mind the direction the winter wind blows and try to ensure it will carry scent to you rather than away! A bonus of evolution to more mild winters is that less frost means more flowers and stronger scent. If space is limited a little pruning will create a more densely flowering shrub. After flowering cut each shoot's extended growth back to two flower buds (these are fat and round - not the long and narrow leaf buds) which will then form flowering sideshoots. Routinely prune out any dead, damaged or crossing branches. As Hamamelis varieties are produced by grafting it is important not to cover the graft union when planting otherwise the rootstock will produce shoots; if this happens remove them at the base. (grafting basically gives a new variety of plant raised from seed, root or softwood cuttings the vigour of a compatible plant noted for strong root development. The graft union is where a bud or stem from the new variety is joined through an incision in the stem of the rooted plant known as the rootstock). Keep Hamamelis watered during dry spells.

VARIETIES:-

H. x intermedia PALLIDA (also known as MOLLIS) - clusters of sulpher-yellow extremely scented flowers. VEZNA has large orange-yellow flowers with pendent petals flushed red at the bases. AURORA - long spidery blooms pale yellow at the tips and warm orange at the bases. JELENA bears large glowing coppery-orange flowers and the slightly hairy leaves turn orange/red in autumn. Not as strongly scented. APHRODITE has orange/yellow sweetly scented blooms on spreading branches. ORANGE PEEL - vigorous the name says it all. DIANE has dark red flowers but not a very strong scent. She looks her best when positioned so that the sun shines through her petals and provides contrast if there are other orange and red varieties in the vicinity. Orange to purple autumn colour. ARNOLD PROMISE - golden-yellow flowers. WESTERSTEDE - strong upright habit with later primrose-yellow flowers.

H. vernalis SANDRA - purple young leaves turning yellow, orange, red and purple in autumn. Purple shoots followed by dark yellow flowers.

CHIMONANTHUS PRAECOX (wintersweet) - vigorous broadly upright shrub. Pendent, sweet scented sulphur-yellow waxy flowers with brownish-purple centres on leafless stems. Petals almost translucent. Followed by glossy mid-green leaves. LUTEUS bears wide-opening clear yellow flowers. Ideal shrub to train against a wall in full sun; in well-drained soil it will grow to 4m (12') high with a 3m (10') spread. The warmth of the wall will encourage ripe wood and prolific flowering.

CERCIS SILIQUASTRUM (Judas tree) - 6m (20') high, 4m (12') across but slow growing. Bears clusters of magenta-pink pea-like flowers in spring. Followed by bronze heart-shaped leaves turning glaucous blue-green and finally yellow in autumn. Grow in full sun or dappled shade in moist but well-drained soil.

FOTHERGILLA GARDENII - 1m (3') high and across with a slender upright growth habit. Oval mid-green leaves turn crimson, red and yellow in autumn. Bottlebrush-like fragrant white flowers borne before the leaves in mid to late spring. Likes soil enriched with organic matter and a sunny position. BLUE MIST has blue-green foliage.

CHAENOMELES (Flowering Quince) - an invaluable source of early flowers. Varieties include:- C. x superba PINK LADY - clusters of cup-shaped dark rose-pink flowers early in the year on bare stems. Glossy mid-green leaves, green fruits maturing to yellow. 1m (3') high and across. CORAL SEA - not surprisingly coral flowers.
C. x speciosa MOERLOOSEI - large white flowers flushed dark pink reminiscent of apple blossom. SIMONII has large double dark blood-red flowers. 1m (3') high, up to 2m (6') across. GEISHA GIRL - bears peach-pink flowers followed by oval glossy dark green leaves on spiny branches with edible fruit. NIVALIS has elegant pure white flowers from February. Vigorous so will need regular pruning. UMBILICATA bears dark pink flowers.

Chaenomeles are suitable as specimen shrubs either in a border or trained against a sunny wall - red brick is an especially attractive background. After flowering prune wall shrubs by cutting back the previous year's growth to two or three buds. Plant in well-drained soil. Shrubs for wall training should be planted away from the wall's rain shadow (and footings) - then directed towards the wall.

VIBURNUM x bodnantense DAWN - erect habit reaching 2.7m (9') high and across. Rose-red buds preceding deliciously scented clusters of tubular sugar-pink flowers on bare branches from November to March. Grow in moist well-drained soil in full sun or partial shade. Every three to four years in March remove some of the older stems so that new wood can ripen for flowering. CHARLES LAMONT bears bright pink flowers.

CORNUS (Dogwood) - C. florida RAINBOW is a flowering dogwood with leaves margined buttercup-yellow turning red-purple with scarlet margins in autumn. Also produces pink/white bracts (a whorl of modified

leaves surrounding a flower). 3m (10') high, 2.5m (8') across.
C. ALBA SIBIRICA (Red-barked dogwood) - in winter the young stems are glowing red which can reach 2m (6½') high. Dark green leaves turn bright red in autumn. In late spring to early summer white flowers are produced which give way to white oval fruits tinged with blue. These should be planted in full sun to ripen the red stems and highlight them in winter. Will do best in a particularly water retentive soil. In March cut stems down to two or three buds from the base to encourage the growth of new stems which have the best colour. ELEGANTISSIMA has grey-green leaves with white margins and red stems by winter.

KERRIA JAPONICA - arching green stems and fresh bright green leaves combined with yellow flowers in springtime. Large and single (3-5cm 1¼-2" across) for GOLDEN GUINEA, large, pompom and double for PLENIFLORA. Vigorous and upright 2m (6') high and across this shrub will grow in well-drained soil in sun or partial shade. After flowering cut back all flowered shoots to new strong growth.

DAPHNE BHOLUA JACQUELINE POSTILL - upright evergreen shrub with extremely fragrant clusters of flowers deep purple-pink outside and white inside from late winter. GURKHA is deciduous and has white flowers flushed purple. Allow space of 1.8m (6') high and 1.5m (5') across for these shrubs. D. MEZEREUM has fragrant purplish-pink flowers on bare spreading stems up to 1.2m (4') high and 1m (3') across. Borne late winter/early spring. Grey-green leaves followed by fleshy round red fruit. ALBA has creamy white flowers followed by yellow fruit. Grow in moist but well-drained soil in sun or shade sheltered from wind. After flowering cut old shoots back to ground level. (For the record birds, especially starlings eat red berries first leaving white, pink, purple and yellow berries on the shrubs for longer. Blackcaps have a preference for white berries.)

JASMINUM NUDIFLORUM (Winter Jasmine) - deciduous with graceful arching green shoots bearing showers of little golden-yellow stars throughout winter into spring. Ideal for a wall growing 3m (10') high and across but will need additional support. After flowering prune out the old growth tying in the new to the support e.g. a trellis panel screwed to the wall. Well-drained soil in sun or partial shade.

GARRYA ELLIPTICA JAMES ROOF - dense, upright evergreen shrub with dark green leathery leaves that are resistant to salt winds. From midwinter into spring festoons of silver-grey catkins up to 20cm (8") long sway to the slightest breeze. They cope well with pruning and training so can be kept considerably more compact than the 4m (12') height and spread that can be reached. Grow in well-drained soil in full sun or partial shade,

LONICERA STANDISHII - an upright deciduous shrub with clusters of tubular fragrant creamy- white flowers on bare stems from late autumn into early spring. Height and spread is 1.2-1.5m (4-5'). Produces red berries. L. x PURPUSII WINTER BEAUTY has red-purple shoots and dark green leaves. Deliciously scented tubular white flowers with prominent yellow tips to the anthers within. Grow in well-drained soil in sun or partial shade.

MAHONIA x MEDIA CHARITY - bears fragrant, deep-yellow flowers in upright spikes between late autumn and late winter. 2.4m (8') high and 1.8m (6') across but can be made more bushy by pinching out the growing tips after flowering. Has leathery dark green shapely evergreen leaves. A shrub for well-drained soil in full or partial shade.

OSMANTHUS DELAVAYI - toothed, leathery, glossy dark green leaves always present. Shows off the clusters of very fragrant white flowers mid to late spring. Followed by oval blue-black fruit. 2m (6') high and up to 3m (10') across. A rounded shrub with arching branches it can be trained against a sheltered wall planted in well-drained soil in sun or partial shade.

SARCOCOCCA CONFUSA (Christmas box) - dense domed-shaped bushy shrub evergreen with tapered glossy, dark green leathery leaves. Clusters of very fragrant white flowers borne in winter followed by round glossy black fruit. 90cm (3') high and 1.2m (4') across. Grow in deep to partial shade in organically enriched moist but well-drained soil.

FORCYTHIA LYNWOOD - broad-petalled rich yellow flowers borne before the leaves early to mid-spring. 3m (10') in height and spread. Plant in moist but well-drained soil in full sun or light dappled shade. As these shrubs flower on the previous year's growth cut back to vigorous upward and outward growing shoots after flowering.

SYRINGA x PERSICA (Persian LILAC) - a bushy shrub with a height and spread of 2m (6'). Has upright clusters of fragrant lilac flowers in late spring. Dark green leaves. ALBA has white flowers. Plant in organically enriched well-drained soil in full sun. Remove faded flowers, weak and crossing branches plus any shoots from the rootstock. Flowers on previous year's growth. When stems lack vigour due to age cut down to within 30-60cm (12-24") of the ground. Thin regrowth and flowers should appear within 2-3 years.

ABUTILON x SUNTENSE RALPH GOULD - a rapid grower to 1.8m-2.4m (6-8') high and across. Upright deciduous shrub with stiff grey furry shoots and soft grey-green toothed leaves. 8cm (3") wide dark violet-blue long-stalked pendent flowers between late spring and early summer. Grow in well-drained soil in full sun. Remove any dead, diseased or damaged growth.

There is an important point to introduce at this stage in making your garden: relating the shrubs under consideration to the trees you have already planted. I call this '**SYMBIOTIC PLANTING**' - the choosing of plants with individual qualities which become reciprocally active on integration. For example PRUNUS SERRULA is noted for its mahogany-like red/brown peeling bark. If HAMAMELIS x INTERMEDIA DIANE is planted nearby her red flowers and P. Serrula's bark will be complimentary. As will the brilliant red stems of CORNUS ALBA SIBIRICA. Bring in DAPHNE BHOLUA JACQUELINE POSTILL with her deep purple-pink flowers (really a pale version of red) for a subtle blend. Remember BETULA ERMANII with its cream-pink peeling bark?; what a background to set off the bright red CORNUS ALBA SIBIRICA. Similarly the dazzling white peeling bark of BETULA UTILIS variety JACQUEMONTII draws attention to the stunning red stems of CORNUS ALBA ELEGANTISSIMA in winter. And compliments the grey-green leaves with white margins of the Cornus in summer.

CHAPTER EIGHT
'SHRUBS - USING AND CHOOSING FOR SUMMER'

'TIM'S CHOICE' for summer begins with CLEMATIS and those known as VITICELLAS. Semi-woody climbers they perform into late summer with an abundance of single, open bell-shaped flowers from deep purple to mauve-blue and rosy-pink to deep red. These are ideal for a SYMBIOTIC PLANTING alongside spring flowering shrubs such as FORCYTHIA, VIBURNUM, HAMAMELIS and CHAENOMELES. So when these shrubs are taking a break their structure can support the flowering CLEMATIS. When the clematis have finished they can be cut back to around 30cm (1') to leave the branches of the host shrubs clear for flowering. Viticellas are rarely affected by clematis wilt.

You will need to plant your clematis about 60cm (2') away from the shrub so both have room to develop. The top of the rootball needs to be 10-15cm (4-6") below ground level to encourage multiple stems and as a safeguard against 'clematis wilt'. (this is caused by an airborne virus which enters the plant through cuts in the bark made earlier by slugs and snails. When established in the stem it blocks the flow of water causing the plant to wilt. If this happens remove the infected growth and hopefully new shoots will emerge from the portion of the stem below ground because the virus is only active above soil level). Dig a hole 45cm (18") square and deep in well-drained soil forking up the base with a few handfuls of Blood Fish and Bone. Soak the plant in a bucket of water for at least 20 minutes and gently loosen the roots as when tree planting. Angle the clematis towards its host placing a stout twig for directional training and backfill with soil enriched with organic material before firming in well. Clematis like a cool root run so place some pieces of roof tile around the plant to retain moisture. Keep watered especially until established. Prune back to two strong leaf buds some 30cm (1') from the ground to encourage vigorous growth. Mulch regularly with organic material.

New clematis plants are easily created. Divert a length of stem along the ground from a reasonably mature plant. Then bury it under 5-8cm (2-3") of moisture retentive soil. After a few months several little plants will have rooted and can be severed and potted up. This is known as LAYERING.

CLEMATIS CIRRHOSA is ideal for growing on a sunny sheltered wall and is recommended for its yellowish-white flowers which are borne throughout winter and look like little lanterns. These are followed by silky seedheads which glisten in sunlight. Variety BALEARICA has evergreen ferny leaves tinged with bronze in winter and nodding bell-shaped cream citrus-scented flowers speckled inside from October to April. FRECKLES bears cream flowers with insides tinged red. These can reach 4.5m (15') but can be contained by pruning IMMEDIATELY after flowering. Remember they flower on the previous season's growth.

Red and blue clematis are especially attractive within the branches of purple leaved shrubs such as COTINUS COGGYGRIA ROYAL PURPLE. Viticellas are ideal but Clematis ETOILE ROSE would be worth considering. From midsumer to autumn it has many nodding, open bell-shaped deep rose-pink flowers some 5cm (2") across in clusters. Furthermore both plants require pruning February to March - the clematis to two strong leaf buds some 45cm (18") from the ground as flowering occurs on new growth, the cotinus requiring the removal of old flowering wood as flowers are borne on two year old wood. A thick mulch of organic material encouraging vigorous regrowth can then be applied. Cotinus is often called the 'smoke bush' because its dense puffs of tiny pink flowers resemble clouds of pink smoke. Royal Purple has dark red-purple foliage (turning shades of gold, orange and scarlet in autumn) which is a perfect foil for the flowers. The oval leaves appear translucent when lit from behind by sunlight. Likes a well-drained soil in full sun to partial shade and will grow up to 2.4m (8') in height and spread.

BUDDLEJAS can also be given added value through a partnership with viticellas, both requiring pruning at the same time. Known as the 'BUTTERFLY BUSH' because the tapering spires of flowers awash with energy-rich nectar are a mecca for all types of butterfly (along with bees and hoverflies) from late summer into autumn. Moths will take over as evening falls. Recommended is LOCHINCH with 20cm (8") spikes of violet flowers each with an orange eye and a lovely vanilla-like fragrance on arching stems. Leaves are mid-green with a white hairy bloom and are deciduous. GLASNEVIN is semi-evergreen with dark green leaves furry white underneath and fragrant dark lilac flowers in 30cm (1') spires. Buddlejas will thrive in reasonable soil in full sun and will make 2.5m (8') of height in a season (in time up to 1.2m (4') in width). However as they flower on the current season's growth it is important to cut back all new shoots to within 5cm (2") of the old wood in February. For appearance spent flowers should be removed and to prevent winter wind damage cut back by

½ after flowering. A real class specimen plant is B. ALTERNIFOLIA with graceful long arching branches bearing dense clusters of highly scented lilac flowers on the previous year's growth in early summer. Leaves are dark green with a silvery tinge. After flowering the stems can be reduced by about ⅓ of their height to healthy buds or non-flowering sideshoots to maintain an attractive shape and to promote flowering wood. Up to 4m (12') in height and spread.

Viticellas can also be used effectively with LAVATERA - known as tree mallows these bear large showy flowers in shades of pink, mauve and white from early summer until autumn. ROSEA grows to 1.7m (5½') in height and spread with a profusion of dark pink funnel-shaped flowers up to 7cm (3") across. BARNSLEY 2m (6') high and in width has similar sized fluted flowers in white with a red centre which mature to soft-pink. Both are semi-evergreen with grey-green leaves. CANDY FLOSS has the same dimensions as Barnsley but with funnel-shaped pale pink flowers to 7cm (3") across. Smaller cultivars include SHORTY with hairy pale green leaves and saucer-shaped white or rose-pink flowers to 5cm (2") across, height and spread of 1m (3'). L. THURINGIACA ICE COOL has snowy buds which open to reveal pure white funnel-shaped long-stalked flowers of intense luminosity. They do not remain on the plant when finished so it always appears particularly fresh. Up to 1.5m (5') in height and spread with grey hairy stems and mid-green rounded leaves with heart-shaped bases. Lavatera are rapid growers and thrive in reasonable soil in full sun and are tolerant of sea breezes. However they rarely last in excess of five years. After flowering reduce the plants by ½ to protect their soft stems from damage by winter winds. In spring when frosts are less likely cut out any weak growths and prune all stems to within 30cm (1') of the ground to encourage strong attractive growth. During the growing season remove any damaged growth to prevent disease. Barnsley is inclined to revert from white to pink so any pink flowered growth should be removed to reduce the chances of this happening.

Every garden should include LAVANDULA or LAVENDER as it is generally known. Its unique scent exuded by both flowers and leaves is beloved of gardeners and perfumeries for generations. (even in winter pinching the leaves releases a scent so evocative of summer). And therefore perfectly suited for edging paths, informal hedges/groups and planting either in the ground or in pots near to doors, windows and seats. From midsummer the flower spikes are rich in nectar and so especially attractive to bees. Lavender grows best in a sunny position and requires just some reasonably fertile very well-drained soil. They will appreciate a handful per square metre/yard of garden lime in spring along with a handful of SULPHATE OF POTASH but no further feeding is required. Ideally plant in spring so the roots can establish digging some horticultural grit into the base of the hole and adding some to the planting soil if on the heavy side. Water until established. Terracotta pots containing lavender look very attractive especially as specimens on paved areas. Pots will need to be 30-38cm (12-15") and filled with a mixture of equal parts John Innes Number 2, multi-purpose compost and horticultural grit (all available at garden centres). A few pieces of broken clay flower pots or similar in the bottom of the pot will improve drainage (see if the garden centre have some if you haven't). Water when the soil surface dries out. During autumn/winter remove to a bright cool place with good air circulation watering at the base when the leaves begin to wilt. In groups plant lavender 30cm (1') apart to allow for spread.

Careful pruning is essential for successful lavender growing. After flowering use your hedge shears or secateurs to remove the faded flowers. Do not hack into the the leaf mass as being evergreen it is protective in winter. Clipping should be done by August to give the resulting new growth time to ripen before cold weather arrives and note that next season's flower buds are beginning to form at this time. Healthy plants can be encouraged to 'bush out' by cutting any straggly growth back to new shoots in spring.

Recommended are LAVANDULA AUGUSTIFOLIA LODDON BLUE 50cm (20") tall with deep blue-purple flowers and grey-green thin leaves. BEECHWOOD BLUE grows to 45cm (18") and is slightly paler. HIDCOTE is a favourite with silver-green leaves and dark purple flowers growing to 60cm (2') high. Another is MUNSTEAD 45cm (18") tall with lighter blue-purple flowers. The French Lavender LAVANDULA STOECHAS is less hardy than its English counterpart so will appreciate a position sheltered from winter cold and dampness. MARSHWOOD is a particularly vigorous hybrid with large purple flower heads topped with pale pink plume-like bracts like rabbit's ears and grey-green leaves. It will reach up to 60cm (2') and will flower from May to September if spent flowers are continually removed.

If you have a wall whose appearance is not particularly attractive you could use a climber often seen in the gardens of stately homes. PARTHENOCISSUS QUINQUEFOLIA known as VIRGINIA

CREEPER. This is a vigorous woody plant which progresses by affixing itself with suckers. After planting attach the shoots to the wall with strong tape which will hold them in place until they grow and produce suckers. Make sure that the mortar in the wall is in good condition otherwise the climber could damage it further. Trim growth from around windows doors and gutters. In spring sunshine glossy unfurling leaves will shimmer, in summer you will have a backdrop of rich green restful foliage to invigorate other plantings. By autumn the leaves composed of 5 oval sharply toothed leaflets (hence 'quinquefolia') will have turned rich crimson. In winter use your shears to cut back growth to the wall.

CISTUS often called SUN or ROCK ROSES come highly recommended for ease of cultivation and their daily display of delicate flowers reminiscent of wild roses or poppies; from early summer to early autumn. Dry, stony or impoverished soil will do but full sun is essential. A wall or paving nearby will reflect warmth and this will help to ripen flowering wood. Ideally plant in spring incorporating some grit into the planting hole and soil to aid drainage if necessary. Be careful not to damage the roots and note that cistus do not like being planted too deeply. There is no need to feed these plants but it is worth keeping a compact bush by initially and from time to time pinching out the growing tips. Pruning is best avoided as cistus do not regrow from old wood. Each flower only lasts a day but there is a continuous supply and the leaves are present throughout the year. SILVER PINK has dark green leaves; grey-green on the undersides. And silvery-pink flowers with almost white centres and golden stamens 8cm (3") across. Grows to 75cm (30") high and 90cm (3') across. PEGGY SAMMONS has grey-green leaves and pale pink flowers with white centres like a wild rose 6cm (2½") across. 1m (3') in height and spread. PURPUREUS has sticky red-flushed shoots and dark green leaves. Flowers are deep pink with purple spots at the base of the petals. 7cm (3") across. Up to 1m (3') high and across. LADANIFER the gum cistus is a large shrub 1.8m (6') high and 1.2m (4') across. The dull green leathery leaves exude a fragrant gum. The large white flowers have bright yellow stamens and crimson blotches at the base of the petals and are up to 10cm (4") across. C. CRISPUS SUNSET has cerise-pink flowers with grey leaves and reaches 60cm (2') in height and spread. CORBARIENSIS bears dark green leaves and red buds which open to white flowers 4cm (1½") across with yellow centres and stamens. 1m (3') high and 1.5m (5') across. C. SALVIIFOLIUS PROSTRATUS grows only to 15-25cm (6-

10") high but spreads to 60-90cm (2-3') making a useful ground cover. Grey-green leaves and white flowers with yellow centres.

A shrub which generates a talking point is CALLICARPA BODINIERI variety GIRALDII PROFUSION. In midsummer it bears clusters of small pale pink flowers which mature to violet berries resembling polished beads by autumn. Known as the 'BEAUTY BERRY' it has deciduous dark green leaves that are bronze on emergence and turn purplish-pink in autumn. An upright shrub to 3m (10') high with a 2.5m (8') spread it likes well-drained soil in sun or partial shade and watering in dry weather. Annually remove up to one in five of the older stems to the base to prevent congestion. Any damaged branches can be cut back to new shoots. For maximum pollination (and therefore berries) plant at least two specimens.

CEANOTHUS CONCHA will bring clouds of brilliant deep blue flowers into your garden. This is a dense evergreen shrub with finely-toothed dark green leaves and arching branches growing up to 3m (10') in height and spread. In late spring a profusion of red buds explode into flower. Grow in full sun on well-drained soil. Best out of strong cold winds although sea breezes are tolerated. Flowers on the previous season's wood so in midsummer prune flowered shoots by ⅓. On young plants encourage a bushy habit by pinching out the growing tips.

Certainly worth growing is WEIGELA PRAECOX VARIEGATA bearing many clusters of star-fish-shaped fragrant pink flowers with yellow throats on arching branches in late spring/early summer. Leaves are dark green with creamy yellow margins which mature to white. Will attain a height of up to 2.5m (8') with a 2m (6') spread in well-drained soil in full sun to partial shade. Some further flowering is possible come late summer. Flowers on previous season's growth so prune stems with faded flowers back to strong upright shoots below. Keep the shrub in shape by shortening any straggly new growth.

ESCALLONIA PEACH BLOSSOM is a vigorous evergreen shrub with glossy dark green leaves. From early to midsummer arching shoots bear short clusters of peach-pink chalice-shaped flowers up to 2.5cm (1") across. Will attain a height of 1.8-2.4m (6-8') with a spread of 1.5-1.8m (5-6'). Likes well-drained soil in full sun and although tolerant of sea breezes escallonia can be troubled by cold drying winds and if these prevail the shrub is best trained against a wall. Annually prune flowered shoots back to young sideshoots which will then produce the wood for next season's flowers. Any straggly growth can be similarly cut back.

For its wonderful fragrance LONICERA or HONEYSUCKLE must be included. It is pollinated by moths so is especially aromatic at night to attract them. (And many garden moths are both delicate and beautifully marked; so unlike the drab brown visitors to forgotton pullovers). L. PERICLYMENUM GRAHAM THOMAS has a lovely spicy scent from masses of tubular 4cm (1½") flowers which mature from white to yellow sometimes with a red flush throughout summer. In autumn these give way to bright red berries. L. PERICLYMENUM SEROTINA bears creamy-white flowers streaked dark red-purple accompanied by a rich fruity fragrance. Both reach a height of up to 7m (22') but are best pruned to strong young growth immediately after flowering which occurs on the previous year's growth. A similar height L. AMERICANA has very fragrant tubular white flowers turning yellow later flushed red-purple 5cm (2") long succeeded by red berries. L. x HECKROTTII is noted for its fragrant tubular flowers 4cm (1½") long pink outside and orange-yellow inside and followed by red berries. Up to 5m (15') high. Honeysuckles are deciduous, the periclymenums have mid-green leaves with glaucous undersides, americana dark green leaves and heckrottii dark green with blue-green underneaths. All are twining climbers and ideal for covering both vertically (walls/fences via trellis) and horizontally (along the ground and through other plants in the mixed border). Plant in moist well-drained soil in full sun or partial shade (which may help to deter aphids - a possible pest).

Commonly known as 'MOCK ORANGE' PHILADELPHUS SYBILLE has graceful arching branches which in midsummer are covered in single cup-shaped orange-scented white flowers with purple marks in the centres up to 5cm (2") across. Attains a height of 1.2m (4') and a spread of 90cm (3'). Will grow in well-drained soil in sun or partial shade. Prune out old wood from the base after flowering leaving room for the new shoots to make next season's flowering wood.

FREMONTODENDRON CALIFORNIA GLORY is a vigorous evergreen shrub growing to 6m (20') with a 4m (12') spread. Among its dark green leaves come saucer-shaped deep yellow glistening flowers 4-6cm (1½-2½") across. Ideal for training against a warm, sunny wall or for the back of the mixed border where it will bloom from late spring until autumn. Will grow in moist well-drained reasonable soil in full sun preferably away from cold drying winds. Basically prune out flowered growth to strong shoots which will then develop and flower later in the season. If against a wall tie in main stems to the wall removing outward growing shoots to sideshoots that will develop parallel to the wall.

TAMARIX RAMOSISSIMA PINK CASCADE is especially suited to seaside gardens and light sandy soils. However it will grow well in moist well-drained soil in full sun ideally out of cold drying winds. Foliage is needle-like giving a feathery appearance and in late summer/ early autumn arching red-brown shoots break into plumes of elegant rich pink flowers 7cm (3") long. To achieve a well-branched multi-stemmed shrub reduce stems by ½ on planting and during the following year. In early spring remove any weak growth and cut back flowered stems to strong sideshoots. Height and spread of 5m (15').

CHAPTER NINE
'ROSES: ESSENCE OF AN ENGLISH GARDEN'

Technically Roses are deciduous or semi-evergreen perennial shrubs and climbers. Aesthetically their flowers are so beautiful and usually so fragrant that their inclusion in gardens over centuries is illustrious. For simplicity 'Tim's Choice' will centre on varieties from four groups - large-flowered (also called hybrid teas), cluster-flowered (also called floribundas), shrub (also known as old or old-fashioned) and climbing/rambling.

Basically you can either buy roses mail-order or from a garden centre or shop where they will be prepackaged or in a pot. As always a dedicated grower has a more extensive range and usually the edge in quality. Obtain a catalogue which will offer helpful illustrations and cultural information. The roses will arrive 'bare rooted' having been lifted from the growing fields. A garden centre generally sells a good selection of roses in pots. This does not necessarily mean that they have actually been grown in the pots - often bare rooted plants will have been stuffed into pots as a convenient short-term measure for transit and display. Shops often sell roses whose bare roots have been enclosed in a polythene bag of moist peat with attractive packaging showing a picture and cultural information. With garden centres and shops you can see before you buy. A rose is a plant for the open ground and the longer it is out of it the more stressed it will become. Prepackaged plants have the shortest 'shelf life' succombing quickly to lack of moisture and fluctuations in light and temperature. Consequently they are priced to sell quickly. So as long as the roots are moist, the stems healthy with no shrivelling or die-back and the buds are not unnaturally extended or pale then a good buy is on the cards. With roses in pots look to see if they appear to have been there a long time. Tell-tale signs are moss on the surface of the soil, engrained rain spattered soil on the sides of the pot, a very obvious 'footprint' where the pot has stood, heavy rain-soaked soil and slugs. Others are loosely anchored plants, a lack of vigour, die-back to the stems and pale leaves perhaps showing signs of disease such as blackspot, mildew or rust. The best rose to buy will have three strong stems. If in flower then you can see if your nose agrees with the description of the scent!

Most varieties of rose are grafted on to deep rooting rootstocks such as the Dog Rose (Rosa Canina) which establishes quickly to provide stability and vigour. A taproot strikes out into the soil and emanating from this are fibrous roots which locate nutrients and moisture sometimes quite a long way from the plant itself.

Roses ideally like a moisture retentive but well-drained organically enriched soil, an open sunny position with a little shade early afternoon along with good air circulation but shelter from cold winds. Basically the lighter your soil the more organic material/well rotted manure will have to be added. Before planting dig in as deep as possible. Then mulch in spring and autumn annually to a depth of 8cm (3") when some Blood, Fish and Bone can also be added. An inoculant of mycorrhizal fungi could be used to aid the development of fine feeder roots and therefore healthier and sturdier bushes. Remember that a sheltered spot will contain the scent and also it is nice to have roses near enough to be able to pull them towards your nose! However the musky fragrance of ramblers can be wafted some distance in the air. Whether your rose is bare rooted, prepackaged or in a pot tease out the roots and cut back any damaged roots shortening long thin roots by ⅓ and soak in water for a few hours. The best time to plant is during spring when plants are at their most active although autumn is quite acceptable. Dig a hole twice the width of the root spread and to a spade depth. Place the rose in the hole ensuring the graft union (where the cultivar joins the rootstock) is about 6cm (2½") below soil level. Spread roots outwards and downwards filling in with soil enriched with some additional organic matter. Firm around the rose with your boot to prevent wind rock. Water well and finish with a 8cm (3") mulch of well rotted manure or organic matter but try to keep it away from the stem base. Although it is wise not to let the ground dry out roots should be encouraged to search for water and that will only happen if they do not get used to regular watering.

After planting remove any growth which is damaged or showing any sign of disease leaving the strongest of any crossing branches. If you are planting in autumn wait until the following spring before pruning further. Then you can prune large-flowered roses back to strong shoots around 10-15cm (4-6") from the ground, cluster-flowered to around 15cm (6") and climbing/rambling to around 30-40cm (12-15"). Do not touch the strong growth of shrub roses but remove any weak, diseased, damaged or crossing stems. Spring planted roses can be pruned like this straight away. Pruning basically keeps roses to a manageable size and attractive shape while encouraging flowering. It is good practice to remove dead, diseased and damaged wood to healthy green wood with white pith as soon as you spot it.

The lovely flower which a rose bears is of course the prelude to a fruit which is known as a 'hip' containing seeds. Some roses develop extremely attractive hips which are a delight in late summer/early autumn sunshine (a delicacy for birds too). However for the majority leaving spent flowers to produce hips would deprive your garden of successive blooms. So when a flower has finished cut it off at the second or third strong bud down the stem with your secateurs (a pleasant job amongst the beauty and fragrance of other blooms still in their prime). Make a sharp, clean cut 5mm (¼") above the bud with an angle sloping away from the bud allowing water to run off. Notice how buds are arranged up the stem. Say the first faces inwards the next will face outwards and so on. If you want an open-centred and rounded shape prune to an outward-facing bud, alternatively if you require shoots to fill in the centre of the bush or to grow upwards prune to an inward-facing bud. Eventually as the rose develops the original stems will become less vigorous and it is likely that when the bush shows signs of life come spring a healthy looking bud or shoot will occur at the base of one of these stems. Remove the old stem 5mm (¼") above the bud or shoot. Cutting back to new buds will stimulate shoots which will then bear flowers. It is a good move to cut back to a bud or sideshoot a stem which is rubbing or will rub against another. Sometimes a rose will produce a shoot without a flower bud. If you shorten this to a lower bud it will quite likely produce a flowering stem. Keep an eye open for any growth from below the graft union or away from the base of the rose (called 'suckers'). The shade of green and shape/texture of the leaves will differ from the cultivar. To prevent the rootstock overpowering the cultivar trace the growth to its source and carefully pull it off.

When buds begin to break in springtime it is time to shorten the stems on established large-flowered roses to healthy outward-facing buds around 20-22cm (8-9") above ground level. This will create a shapely open-centred bush allowing air to circulate freely lessening the chances of powdery mildew occuring (a white fungal growth on leaves). So will a 8cm (3") mulch of moisture retaining organic material put down around the plants. This will also help to prevent blackspot - a disease recognised by not surprisingly black spots on the leaves which can lead to leaf loss preventing the manufacture of plant foods. A mulch will act as a barrier stopping blackspot spores from entering the soil and remaining there until next season when they can be activated by warm, wet weather especially if the soil is short of potash. A springtime topdressing of a high potash balanced proprietary rose fertiliser will be beneficial but avoid applying any nitrogen rich foods which promote soft growth attractive to aphids (greenfly). If aphids become too much for natural predators such as blue tits, sparrows and ladybirds to cope with then use one of the organic fatty acid sprays, rub them out with your fingers or suck them up with a battery powered car vacuum cleaner! A nut-feeder nearby will ensure a good number of birds who will appreciate any aphids on offer. Cluster-flowered roses are treated the same as the large-flowered except that they are shortened to around 25-30cm (10-12") from ground level. Individual spent flowers within the cluster can be removed if desired and when the whole cluster has finished it can be removed down to a healthy bud. If there is no obvious bud then cut to a reasonable height in the hope that a dormant bud will be triggered into growth.

Shrub roses differ from the large-flowered and cluster-flowered in that they generally flower on older wood. Therefore in springtime lightly prune back any overlong stems along with any dead, damaged, diseased, weak and crossing growth while maintaining a balanced shape. Prune weak stems harder to stimulate vigorous regrowth. When stems become woody and less vigorous remove them. If practical deadheading these roses without touching the leaves can promote new flowers. If your shrub rose is described as an alba, damask, moss, bourbon, china or portland then prune the main stems back by ⅓ reducing sidegrowths by ⅓ to strong, healthy outward-facing shoots or buds. Remove any very low growth which is brushing the ground. In the autumn cut back any very long stems to prevent wind damage. In the case of shrub roses described as gallicas thin out growth after flowering has finished come midsummer by pruning back sidegrowths to the main stem or to a shoot close to the main stem. When stems become woody and less vigorous remove them at ground level. With hybrid musks cut the main stems back by ⅓ and the sidegrowths by ½. If your rose has lax growth then the lower growth can be gathered together with strong twine and tied to two stakes either side of the rose.

Climbers and ramblers look especially attractive when grown against walls and fences. Prior to planting get some vine eyes and strong galvanised wire from the garden centre. Secure the first wire 45cm (18") from the ground and subsequent wires 30cm (1') above. The wire should be strung 8cm (3") away from the wall/fence through the vine eyes. Plant the rose 30cm (1') from the wall/fence with the roots going away from it towards open ground. Guide the shoots towards the wire with canes if necessary. It is a good idea to prune in autumn and secure growth before the onset of winter winds. It is important to deadhead regularly and tie in new growth throughout the season. The aim of pruning is to create a fan from the main stems and train the sidegrowths outwards. When you buy your climber you will notice it has longer shoots than your other roses so leave them alone apart from cutting back to the first strong outward-facing bud on the outer stems to encourage sidegrowths. Where possible tie in these growths to a horizontal position along the wires. Remove any dead, diseased, damaged or spindly growth and where main shoots fail to branch prune them by 5-8cm (2-3") with an angled cut above bud or leaf to stimulate it. Tying in sideshoots horizontally encourages buds to form shoots which will grow vertically and bear flowers. Train to cover the lower part of the wall first. Training is a constant process and it is always easier to guide and tie in growth when it is new and pliable. When the climber is established prune the flowered shoots by ⅔ with angled cuts above a healthy shoot or bud in autumn. Keep growth tied in and watch out for any shoots that are rubbing together. Prune old woody growth back to a healthy shoot and tie in or to a strong bud.

Ramblers provide a garden with colourful height and are especially suited to being trained as a screen or feature such as a rose arch. They produce a profusion of long flexible stems near to the ground which lend themselves to horizontal training. Flowering occurs on the previous year's wood. On planting aim to stimulate growth from the base by cutting back to 40cm (16") from the ground removing any dead, damaged and weak growth. Fan out the shoots horizontally in the direction you want. When the desired area has been covered you can shorten sideshoots by ⅔ after flowering, removing surplus growth altogether so that flowering sideshoots can develop for next season. Secure new growth as it is made to the framework with ties or twine bearing in mind that the stems will thicken. Eventually remove older woody stems to the base to encourage new growth. Be careful not to damage the plant by tugging out a long piece of woody growth; remove it carefully by making several cuts along the length and removing a little bit at a time. If you want to restrict growth say in a small garden all flowered stems can be cut away and new ones tied in. In springtime give the rose a good mulch and feed. An ideal base for a screen is a chainlink fence allowing easy tying in and giving good air circulation. Vertical growth can be achieved by training shoots upwards and then tying in. A rose arch is an attractive feature to incorporate over a pathway bringing the colour, beauty and scent of the rose to every trip along the garden path. For the DIY challenged there are plenty of ready-made wooden and metal arches available from garden centres or alternatively rustic poles and trellis for individual design and construction. Remember as with fences an arch needs to be well made from durable well-preserved materials with over-the-top anchorage to cope with the weight of a mature rose in a strong wind. You will need a rose either side of the arch planted on the outside so the growth does not restrict the pathway. A wider arch allows shoots to be directed as per wall training and then drawn with their sidegrowths over the top of the arch. Keep growth within the shape of the arch paying close attention to tying in and shortening vigorous upright and outward-growing shoots. The objective is always to have the structure evenly and copiously covered with flowers and foliage. Training shoots horizontally encourages this. If the arch is narrow shoots can be trained so they come back on themselves at a higher level eventually giving a snake-like effect from the bottom to the top of the arch side. This achieves the maximum flowering potential from continuous horizontal growth covering the complete side. Alternatively the shoots could be wound round in a spiral from bottom to top. Tying in to vine eyes and wires on the arch minimises the chance of stems chafing on the structure.

It is not recommended to plant roses where old roses have been removed. During the life of a rose fungal parasites gradually build up on the roots. A mature and healthy root system is unaffected by this but the parasites will remain in the soil at quite a high level after the rose has been taken out. If a new rose is introduced the parasites will be too strong for a developing root system to tolerate and the rose will rapidly lose vigour. A way round this is to dig a hole big enough to take a cardboard box and plant the new rose in fresh soil within the box. By the time the roots have ventured beyond the confines of the decomposing box they will be strong enough to cope with any residual fungal parasites. Alternatively use an inoculant of mycorrhizal fungi.

Roses can be grown successfully in pots no smaller than 10 litres but they will need to be treated differently to those planted in open ground. Firstly prune the roots by shortening the dominant ones which will encourage them to fan out and build a strong fibrous root system which can then use the whole contents of the pot as a workplace. You can use a proprietary rose and shrub compost from the garden centre along with a rose fertiliser. A mulch will be beneficial. Every other year repot the rose into fresh compost and if certain roots have hit the dead end of the bottom of the pot prune them to encourage the production of new fibrous feeding roots.

And if you decide to cut some roses for a vase cut them at an angle and then plunge the stems into boiling water; count to ten and then plunge into cold water - this apparently shocks them into lasting longer!

TIM'S CHOICE:-
LARGE -FLOWERED ROSES

FRAGRANT CLOUD - powerfully scented deep pink flowers 75cm (30") high, 60cm (24") wide.

WENDY CUSSONS - another very fragrant deep pink 1m (3') high, 70cm (28") wide.

ALEC'S RED - richly perfumed crimson flowers 1m (3') high, 70cm (28") wide.

WHISKY MAC - very fragrant apricot flowers 75cm (30") high, 60cm (24") wide.

PAUL SHIRVILLE - strong sweet fragranced rose-pink flowers 1m (3') high, 75cm (30") wide.

ERNEST H MORSE - very fragrant crimson flowers 75cm (30") high, 60cm (24") wide.

JUST JOEY - fragrant copper-orange flowers with wavy margins 75cm (30") high, 70cm (28") wide.

ROYAL WILLIAM - velvety deep red fragrant flowers 1m (3') high, 75cm (30") wide.

BLESSINGS - fragrant coral-pink flowers 1.1m (3½') high, 75cm (30") wide.

ALEXANDER - noted for its luminescent orange-vermilion flowers rather than scent 1.5m (5') high, 80cm (32") wide.

FREEDOM - fragrant bright yellow flowers 75cm (30") high, 60cm (24") across.

PEACE - pale yellow blooms edged with cerise-pink, slightly fragrant. 1.2m (4') high, 1m (3') wide.

ELINA - fragrant ivory-white flowers with lemon-yellow centres 1.1m (3½') high, 75cm (30") wide.
SILVER JUBILEE - rose-pink fragrant flowers shaded salmon-pink 1.1m (3½') high, 60cm (24") wide.
SIMBA - slightly fragrant light yellow blooms 60cm (24") high, 50cm (20") wide.
TROIKA - fragrant orange shaded red flowers 1m (3') high, 75cm (30") wide.
ALPINE SUNSET - peach-pink flowers flushed creamy-yellow and very fragrant 60cm (24") high and wide.
POLAR STAR - not fragrant but lovely creamy-white flowers 1m (3') high, 70cm (28") wide.
ROSE GAUJARD - cherry-red blooms silvery-pink underneath and slightly fragrant. 1m (3') high, 75cm (30") wide.
PINK FAVOURITE - slightly fragrant deep pink flowers 75cm (30") high, 60cm (24") wide.
DEEP SECRET - very fragrant deep crimson flowers 1m (3') high, 75cm (30") wide.
DUTCH GOLD - golden yellow very fragrant blooms 1.1m (3½') high, 75cm (30") wide.

CLUSTER-FLOWERED ROSES
MARGARET MERRIL - very fragrant white tinged pink flowers 80cm (32") high, 60cm (24") wide.
AMBER QUEEN - fragrant amber-yellow blooms 50cm (20") high, 60cm (24") wide.
KORRESIA - fragrant bright yellow flowers 75cm (30") high, 60cm (24") wide.
MOUNTBATTEN - fragrant pale yellow flowers 1.2m (4') high, 75cm (30") wide.
ARTHUR BELL - extremely fragrant golden yellow blooms 1m (3') high, 60cm (24") wide.
SOUTHAMPTON - fragrant apricot blooms flushed scarlet 1.1m (3½') high, 70cm (28") wide.
FRAGRANT DELIGHT - very fragrant coppery flowers tinged yellow 1m (3') high, 75cm (30") wide.
CHINATOWN - fragrant yellow flowers 1.2m (4') high, 1m (3') wide.
FLOWER CARPET - series including rose-pink, yellow and white 75cm

(30") high, 1.2m (4') wide.

GRUSS AN AACHEN - scented soft creamy-pink blooms 45cm (18") high and wide.

ICEBERG - pure white to cream slightly fragrant blooms 80cm (32") high, 65cm (26") wide.

SHRUB ROSES

BONICA 82 - fragrant sprays of rose-pink flowers 85cm (34") high, 1.1m (3½') wide.

BELLE DE CRÉCY - gallica bearing fragrant purple-red maturing to violet flowers. Greyish-green leaves. 1.2m (4') high, 1m (3') wide.

CARDINAL DE RICHELIEU - gallica with fragrant deep burgundy flowers 1m (3') high, 1.2m (4') wide.

CHARLES DE MILLS - gallica bearing fragrant crimson flowers, 1.2m (4') in height and width.

ROSA MUNDI - an unscented gallica with crimson blooms striped white, 1.2m (4') in height and width.

GERTRUDE JEKYLL - deep pink flowers with a classic fragrance. Greyish-green leaves.1.5m (5') high, 1m (3') wide.

FERDINAND PICHARD - a hybrid perpetual with fragrant pale pink flowers striped crimson and purple 1.5m (5') high, 1.2m (4') wide.

ALBA MAXIMA - the actual White Rose of Yorkshire. Creamy-white fragrant flowers. Greyish-green leaves. 2.2m (7') high, 1.5m (5') wide.

FÉLICITÉ PARMENTIER - an alba with blush-pink flowers 5m (15') high, 4m (12') wide.

MADAME LEGRAS DE ST GERMAIN - an alba with fragrant lemon-white blooms. Greyish-green leaves. 2m (6') high and wide. Can be used as a climber where it will attain a height of 5m (15').

MAIDEN'S BLUSH - alba with sweet scented blush-pink flowers. Bluish-green leaves. 1.2m (4') high, 90cm (36") wide.

KÖNIGIN VON DÄNEMARK - an alba with very fragrant pink flowers which deepen towards the centres. Bluish-green leaves.1.5m (5') high and 1.2m (4') wide.

ISPAHAN - a damask rose with bright pink fragrant flowers. Grey-green leaves.1.5m (5') high, 1.2m (4') wide.

LA VILLE DE BRUXELLES - a damask with rich pink scented blooms 1.5m (5') high, 90cm (3') wide.

MADAME HARDY - a damask bearing fragrant pure white flowers with green centres 1.5m (5') high, 1.2m (4') wide.

MADAME ISAAC PEREIRE - a bourbon with deep carmine-pink fragrant flowers 2.2m (7') high, 2m (6') wide.

OLD BLUSH - a china rose with slightly fragrant silvery-pink flowers flushed crimson 1.5m (5') high, 1.2m (4') wide.

ZÉPHIRINE DROUHIN - bourbon with scented carmine-pink blooms 3m (10') high, 2m (6') wide. Suitable as a climber too, especially over arches as it is thornless.

FRED LOADS - orange-vermilion flowers with a sweet fragrance 1.8m (6') high, 1.2m (4') wide.

FANTIN-LATOUR - a centifolia rose with blush-pink flowers with green centres 1.5m (5') high, 1.2m (4') wide.

ROSERAIE DE L'HAY - a rugosa rose with richly scented red-purple flowers 2.2m (7') high, 2m (6') wide.

MADAME KNORR - a portland rose bearing fragrant pink flowers darker towards the centre, 1.2m (4') high and 1m (3') wide.

ROSA GALLICA OFFICINALIS - the actual Red Rose of Lancashire although the colour is more pinky-red, scented 80cm (32") high, 1m (3') wide.

SOUVENIR DE LA MALMAISON - a bourbon bearing spicy pearl-pink flowers 1.5m (5') high and wide.

COMMANDANT BEAUREPAIRE - bourbon with fragrant pink flowers striped purple and white 1.2m (4') high and wide.

MADAME PIERRE OGER - bourbon with scented creamy-pink flowers shaded lilac 2m (6') high, 1.2m (4') wide.

BOULE DE NEIGE - bourbon bearing fragrant white flowers with a hint of pink 1.5m (5') high, 1.2m (4') wide.

LOUISE ODIER - bourbon with fragrant rich pink blooms shaded lilac. Light grey-green leaves. 2m (6') high, 1.2m (4') wide.

GLAUCA - delicate cerise-pink flowers fading to pale pink at the centres with gold stamens. Noted for its dark maroon hips and leaves the colour of weathered copper. 2m (6') high, 1.5m (5') wide.

NUTKANA PLENA - bears deep pink flowers edged silvery-pink followed by purplish-red hips which last into winter. 3m (10') high and 1.2-2m (4-6') wide.

MOYESII GERANIUM - blood-red flowers with cream stamens followed by large bottle-shaped orange-red hips. 2.5m (8') high and 1.5m (5') wide.

HIGHDOWNENSIS has deep pink flowers with yellow stamens succeeded

by scarlet flask-shaped hips. 3m (10') high and 2m (6') wide.
GRAHAM THOMAS - scented deep yellow flowers 1.2m (4') high and 1.5m (5') wide.
MARCHESA BOCCELLA - portland with silvery-pink fragrant flowers 1.2m (4') high, 1m (3') wide.
LADY HILLINGDON - a moss rose so-called because of the moss-like growth on the bristly stems. Yolky-yellow scented flowers 90cm (3') high and 60cm (2') wide.
CANTABRIGIENSIS - papery pale yellow flowers and light green ferny foliage on arching reddish stems. Up to 3m (10') in height and width.
CÉLESTE - an alba with fragrant shell-pink flowers with golden-yellow stamens. Relatively thorn free so suitable for training over an arch. Grey-green foliage. 1.5m (5') high and 1.2m (4') wide.
COMPLICATA - gallica with pink flowers fading to white towards the centres and golden stamens. Greyish-green leaves. 2.2m (7') high and 2.5m (8') wide.
FRÜHLINGSGOLD - golden-yellow flowers fade to primrose-yellow. 2.5m (8') high and 2.2m (7') wide.
FRU DAGMAR HASTRUP - rugosa bearing clove-scented pale pink scented flowers with creamy-yellow stamens followed by dark red hips like mini tomatoes. 1m (3') high and 1.2m (4') wide.

CLIMBERS AND (SC)RAMBLERS!

PHYLLIS BIDE - climber with fragrant clusters of yellow flushed pink flowers ideal for an archway. 2.5m (8') high and 1.5m (5') wide. (Very attractive when associated with HONEYSUCKLE).
COMPASSION - climber bearing very fragrant apricot-pink blooms. 3m (10') high and 2.5m (8') wide.
NEW DAWN - climber with clusters of fragrant shell-pink flowers. 3m (10') high and 2.5m (8') wide.
GOLDEN SHOWERS - climber with fragrant bright yellow flowers and few thorns. 3m (10') high and 2m (6') wide.
ALBERTINE - rambler bearing sweetly scented pink blooms with a hint of salmon. 5m (15') high and 4m (12') wide.
MAIGOLD - climber with golden-yellow scented flowers mainly in early summer. 2.5m (8') in height and width.
MADAME GRÉGOIRE STAECHELIN - climber with very fragrant ruffled pink shaded crimson flowers. Succeeded by large round red hips.

6m (20') high and 4m (12') wide.
MORNING JEWEL - climber bearing clusters of deep pink scented flowers. 3m (10') high and 2.5m (8') wide.
BREATH OF LIFE - climber with scented apricot flowers. 2.5m (8') high and 2.2m (7') wide.
MADAME ALFRED CARRIÈRE - a noisette climbing rose with sweetly scented pale pink to cream flowers. 5m (15') high and 3m (10') wide.
SUMMER WINE - climber with scented coral-pink flowers shaded yellow at the bases and large red stamens. 3m (10') high and 2.2m (7') wide.
CLIMBING ETOILE DE HOLLANDE - very fragrant deep red flowers 6m (20') high and 5m (15') wide.
RAMBLING RECTOR - not surprisingly a rambler with musk-scented creamy-white flowers with golden stamens. Grey-green foliage and round orange hips. 6m (20') in height and width.
ALBÉRIC BARBIER - rambler with clusters of slightly fragrant creamy-white flowers. 5m (15') high and 3m (10') wide.
CLIMBING CÉCILE BRUNNER - delicate little light pink flowers with a slight fragrance. 4m (12') in height and width.
BLUSH RAMBLER - clusters of lightly scented shell-pink flowers, fairly thornless. 4m (12') high and 5m (15') wide.
EMILY GRAY - rambler with butter-yellow scented flowers in clusters. 5m (15') high and 3m (10') wide.
CLIMBING ICEBERG - clusters of slightly fragrant white flowers. 3m (10') high and wide.

SYMBIOTIC PLANTING:-

Remember PHILADELPHUS SYBILLE?; planting the deeper coloured shrub roses nearby contrasts wonderfully with the white flowers and their purple marked centres. And inhale a heavenly scent! Roses with bluey-grey/green foliage combine well with the leaves of CISTUS and obviously so do the flowers of this ROCK ROSE. Similarly these roses blend well with LAVENDER producing a real cottage garden scent! COTINUS COGGYGRIA ROYAL PURPLE is a fantastic background for red and purple roses. BUDDLEJAS meld with many different rose colours while LONICERA PERICLYMENUM SEROTINA with its creamy-white flowers streaked dark red-purple makes a perfect partner for red and purple roses. Bring Lavender into the picture here and the scent will be quite wonderful! The VITICELLA CLEMATIS can be put to effective use among roses especially with the climbers and ramblers. Consider ROYAL VELOURS with velvety purple flowers, ETOILE VIOLETTE bearing violet-purple flowers, ABUNDANCE; wine-red flowers, PURPUREA PLENA ELEGANS; violet purple and POLISH SPIRIT; rich purple-blue.

CHAPTER TEN
'PERENNIALS - SEASONED PERFORMERS YEAR AFTER YEAR'
TIM'S CHOICE PART 1

"A damn good buy" as a local shopkeeper would have put it. These are the plants whose colour, texture, shape, form and scent are at the heart of any mixed border. Their ability to survive winter without protection means they are often called 'hardy plants'. If you can find a nursery in your area specialising in hardy plants then this should be your first port of call. Such places are often only open from March to September when perennials are in active growth. This means you can give the plant a health check and perhaps see it in flower. Do not be afraid to hold the plant at the base and lift it out of the pot to inspect the roots. If you see any curled wrinkled creamy-white grubs with tanned heads then walk away; these are VINE WEEVIL larvae. For the record adult vine weevils are blackish beetles about 1cm (½") long with gingery flecks and antennae bent at an angle. They especially target potted plants by night and leave lower leaves with irregular notches around the edges. Ultimately they lay their eggs on the surface of the pot soil and the resulting larvae feed on the roots causing lack of vigour, wilting and eventually death. If later on you decide to have some plants in pots go out after dark shining a light into the plants giving them a little shake. Any vine weevils at work will fall off and can be crunched underfoot. By day check underneath the pots and give any lurkers the same treatment! A top-dressing of sharp gravel will help to prevent vine weevils accessing the soil surface. So will a band of Vaseline around the rim of the pot.

There is a good lesson to be learned from being in a hardy plant nursery. You are likely to come across an area with some cracking mature plants marked 'Not for Sale'. These are the nursery's 'stock plants' which have provided the cuttings that have grown into the plants you have been mulling over. For the majority of hardy plants turning one plant into several is really quite easy and a shrewd and enjoyable way of making a purchase fill more than one planting hole in the long run. Basically the pricing of perennials is determined by the size of the plant - time is money so a bigger plant reflects the duration the grower has had to look after it from taking the cutting together with the cost of pots and soil along the way. A perennial generally increases in size by moving outwards from the centre with new roots and shoots. The chances are that the plant you are looking at can have these new growths teased away and potted up separately. Many gardeners who open their gardens to the public propagate plants in this way and perusal of the plant sales table will often yield some quality plants a little cheaper than nurseries. A plant bought from the person who has actually grown it often comes with an invaluable free gift - advice based on experience.

Garden centres are an alternative source. However perennials will just be one line among all the other components of gardening. So the range is unlikely to be as extensive as a dedicated nursery. They probably will not actually grow the plants but buy them from a grower which means the price reflects at least two profits and transport costs (the environment paying for the latter as well). There is the question of where the grower is based. Many garden centres obtain plants from countries whose climates allow plants to gain ground on those grown in the British Isles. Or from growers at home who use polythene tunnels. Garden centres want to stop people in their tracks with aspects of the next seasonal event; perennials showing lush growth, perhaps buds and the odd flower will fire people's enthusiasm on a bright chilly Sunday afternoon in early spring. Unfortunately growing plants in cushy conditions produces tissue with large thin-walled cells which are easily damaged when subjected to the real-time conditions of the open border; leaving the plants vulnerable to disease and pests. Garden centres of course are open throughout the year meaning that perennials are available during their dormancy. Without growth it is impossible to determine the health of a plant or if in fact it is still alive. Staff at these places can be knowledgeable and helpful or simply programmed to bag purchases and give change! Both nurseries and garden centres generally arrange plants in alphabetical order which makes location easy. As for labels pictures are helpful, dimensions approximate (determined by your soil and growing conditions) and cultural instructions sketchy (symbolic ones half-baked). Just keep it with the plant so you know who's who!

A few perennials can often be seen for sale outside greengrocers and ironmongers. With space at a premium these plants (probably bought from a small-time grower) are likely to be smaller than those at nurseries and garden centres and consequently cheaper. So long as they are healthy and not in advance of those already growing in gardens then they are certainly worth considering. Obviously you will not get the immediate impact of a more mature plant and will have to bide time before teasing away rooted cuttings (a potato peeler is a good tool to use) but your money will go further and perennials are relatively quick to establish. Hardy plants encased in attractive packaging and priced to sell in supermarkets are really only worth considering if they are fresh in; they can soon show the ill-effects of fluctuating light, temperature and under/over watering by inexperienced staff.

Then there is mail order with catalogues and advertisements often depicting borders in exuberant colours with the participating plants available in specially priced collections. The plants will be small enough generally to be practically and economically delivered by post or courier. On arrival it might be best to individually pot them up and look after them until they have made some headway top and bottom before planting out. Be patient - the plants in that fabulous border are a lot further down maturity road than what you have been sent.

Lastly there are 'plant fairs' and shows. These bring together nurseries specialising in all sorts of plants from all over the country which is a great opportunity for choice and advice from places you would probably never get to. If they have created a display garden be aware that it is a 'shop window' for as many of their plants as possible with prizewinning impact (and impulse buying) in mind. In reality the combinations would probably not be possible due to the plants requiring different conditions. Or because the growers have erased the seasonal differences by 'bringing plants on' or 'holding them back'. Be careful at early shows not to buy plants ahead of their normal development outside.

Wherever you buy from if you do the right thing and the plant fails to grow tackle them for a replacement/refund. Most garden centres and mail order firms give guarantees and nurseries are usually accomodating in the interest of future custom.

What every perennial wants when it is given the freedom of the border is warm, moist soil. So any time from late spring/early summer but no later than early autumn. Only in these conditions can roots venture beyond the planting hole and establish a system capable of sustaining good growth above ground. A mulch not only retains moisture but also acts as an insulator keeping the soil warmer for longer. Late spring/early summer plantings almost certainly will need watering from time to time, early autumn ones in decreasing temperatures less so.

How many plants initially go into your mixed border could well be determined by the amount of money you are prepared to spend. However if money was not an issue a 'trolley dash' around nurseries and garden centres would rarely be a wise move. Because the success of any new planting depends on the amount of time a gardener has to look after it and the suitability of the garden itself. Plants are undoubtedly sirens; every year even accomplished gardeners are tempted beyond their better judgement - accumulating plants that will only ever languish in their pots due to lack of time and space. An empty border actually has far less space for planting than it appears; you have to see the plants not as they are in the nursery but as mature clumps. Think bear not cub! Start with a selection of plants to begin a unity/contrast of colour, texture, scent, form, shape and size. Foliage should not be overlooked - its colour, texture and shape is evident before and after flowers. Consider the proportion of plants to each other with a view to having the tallest at the back of the border with a gradual drop in height ending with the shortest at the edge. With 'island beds' the tallest plants should be in the centre - their height being roughly no more than half the width of the bed. Moving from small flowered plants near the house to ones with larger flowers at the end of the garden creates an illusion of greater length. Bear in mind the future maintenance of individual plants and the border as a whole. Choose sturdy plants which are of interest for long periods. A natural look is achieved through planting in groups.

Making a mixed border should never be hurried. Gradually introduce new plants as and when you come across them, can afford them and always when you have time for them. It will become a 'living diary' with plants from many places and people. A big advantage of perennials is that they can be rearranged as the border develops (late summer/early autumn is a good time). In fact the majority will require lifting with a spade from time to time and the new growths teased away with a fork to be replanted or exchanged for something else with a fellow gardener. Perhaps even sold for charity or to finance new acquisitions!

ANNEX: 'TOOL UP'.

Time to buy a WATERING CAN! Now that smaller plants are being introduced into the garden a watering can will make it easier to direct water at those who need it without soaking those who don't! Cans are made from either galvanised steel or plastic. As always quality of material and construction comes at a higher price. Recommended are cans made by HAWS. Galvanised steel cans last a lifetime and more but are heavier to use than plastic which will eventually break after many years of service. A can with a long spout enables you to reach plants further away from you. Cans come with an attachment for the spout called a 'rose' which pointed upwards gives a fine gentle spray while downwards produces more of a heavy shower. Perennials will generally be planted in a hole dug with your trowel. As with all plants make sure the rootball is moist and that the plant sits comfortably in the hole so that the backfilled soil will just cover the top surface of the rootball. Use a dining fork to tease the roots out of their round and round the pot direction so that they will strike out into the surrounding soil. Filling the hole with water prior to planting will help to give the plant a good start. When watering subsequently aim the spout of the can at the base of the plant and give it a thorough soak - this is much more beneficial than little sprinklings. Do this either early in the morning or later in the evening when the soil is cool or cooling and able to absorb the water. See if you can connect WATER BUTTS to your downpipes to save rainwater from the gutters. Good for plants, reservoirs and those on water meters!

TIM'S CHOICE:-

ACHILLEA - the flowers are large and flat-topped overshadowing the stems; when viewed a little way back squatted down they look like little flying-saucers hovering over the border! A. CORONATION GOLD has golden-yellow flowerheads up to 10cm (4") across with silvery-grey ferny leaves on stems 75-90cm (30-36") high from mid-summer to early autumn. Happy in most soils and conditions but best in moist well-drained soil with full sun.

ACONITUM - frightfully toxic if any part is eaten and a favourite of poisoners through time! However BRESSINGHAM SPIRE is worth including for its lovely indigo-blue flowers which resemble monk's hoods (the plant's common name). These are borne on erect stems 90cm (3') high with glossy dark green palm-shaped leaves. Grow ideally in moist soil with shade although other soils and full sun will be acceptable. Performs from mid-summer to early autumn.

AGAPANTHUS - Translated from the Greek; 'agape' - love, 'anthos' - flower so the 'flower of love'. Ideal either for an open sunny spot in moist well-drained soil or large pots (starting 20-22 cm (8-9") filled with John Innes compost Number 3. They make bold clumps with arching strap-shaped leaves from which emerge stout flower stems which bend with the wind. At the top of each stem is a starburst of flowers from white to silver-grey, pale and mid-blues to darker violet inky-blues and purple according to the variety. Will appreciate a mulch of organic matter especially in autumn when the leaves die down to help protect the crowns in winter. Also some slow-release fertiliser at the initial planting. Agapanthus make striking specimen plants if given enough space to mature and look especially attractive in small groups. With potted plants repot into slightly larger pots each year until it becomes impractical; then either plant them in the garden or divide into individuals by pulling the crowns apart using a handfork and plenty of strength! A high potash feed such as that recommended for tomatoes would be beneficial until the flowers show colour and potted agapanthus need plenty of water. During the winter place in a dry sheltered position. A. CASTLE OF MEY at 60cm (24") high with deep blue flowers mid to late summer and BLUE MOON the same height with pale blue flowers in late summer/early autumn are ideal for pots. A. CAMPANULATUS ISIS has dark blue flowers 75cm (30") high mid to late summer. HEADBOURNE HYBRIDS bears soft-blue flowers and reaches 60cm (24"). BLUE GIANT is noted for its rich blue flowers mid to late summer on 1.2m (4') stems. BEN HOPE is the same height with dark blue flowers. LOCH HOPE is a strong grower bearing azure blue flowers up to 100cm (39") high late summer/early autumn. BRESSINGHAM WHITE has pure white flowers mid to late summer reaching a height of 90cm (36"). ANGELA grows strongly to 1.2m (40") with sky-blue drooping flowers while WINDSOR GREY has pale greyish-white flowers with violet tints up to 110cm (43"). LILAC TIME reaches 95cm (37") high.

ALCEA - known universally as the HOLLYHOCK whose towering spires are present in virtually all illustrations of cottage gardens! Technically they are biennials but are best treated as fairly short-lived perennials. Watch out for rust on the leaves and remove any infected ones and destroy them to combat further infection. Will flourish in full sun in well-drained soil. A. ROSEA CHATER'S DOUBLE is a good bet with shades of apricot, pale yellow, scarlet, pink, lavender-blue, purple and white. Hollyhocks reach up to 240cm (8'). A later chapter will cover growing plants from seed and hollyhocks are a species which are easily raised this way. Check out some of the many varieties you can buy from the seed section at garden centres. Hollyhocks produce a lot of seed many of which will germinate in your border; however when they flower during their second year they may well be different to the colours you have enjoyed previously. This comes from 'cross pollination' where the pollen of one colour has been transferred by an insect to the pollen of another colour resulting in seed with the potential to produce a plant of a different hue to either of the parents. Seeing what comes up 'for free' is fun and random 'self-sets' add naturalistic value to the garden. Note 'rosea' - 'rose like' in the name and plant with ROSES and HONEYSUCKLE for time honoured effect.

ALCHEMILLA - popularly called 'LADY'S MANTLE' variety MOLLIS grows up to 45cm (18") in well-drained soil in sun or partial shade. Forms nice clumps of round pale green soft downy leaves with scalloped edges which emit stems of frothy greeny-yellow flowers early summer to early autumn. The leaves look especially attractive after rain when they hold raindrops like little jewels. Interestingly when the leaves are moved by the breeze the raindrops are directed towards the stem; run down and moisten the soil! This plant seeds prolifically and although self-sets can be used throughout the garden blurring the edges of borders and paving, blending with ROSES (especially white ones) and LAVENDER and replacing old woody plants, cutting them to the ground leaves and all before they set seed will avoid a surplus of A.mollis! And likely stimulate fresh flowers and foliage for later in the season. A. ALPINA has the added attraction of silver fringed deep green leaves undercoated with tiny silver hairs which give the plant a shimmering appearance. With similar chartreuse flowers it reaches just 30cm (1') high.

ALLIUM - these are bulbous perennials which can either be bought growing in pots during spring or as dry bulbs during autumn. Either way the bulbs need to be planted roughly 4x the bulb's diameter in well-drained soil in full sun out of the wind. In heavier soil add some horticultural grit to the planting holes. For impact plant in groups of five. Recommended are PURPLE SENSATION at 1m (3') high with an 8cm (3") starburst of deep violet flowers at the top of each stem come summer. Attractive in the dappled shade of SILVER BIRCH. GLOBEMASTER has spheres of violet-purple flowers some 15-20cm (6-8") across on 80cm (32") stems. Both look nice with SHRUB ROSES such as MADAME ISAAC PEREIRE, some of the RUGOSAS and LAVENDER. CRISTOPHII' 30-60cm (12-24") high bears 20cm (8") globes of sparkling metallic purple-pink flowers which gradually open over a period of weeks. The resulting seedhead dries to a bleached white star which sparkles in glancing light and frost. Blends well with ALCHEMILLA MOLLIS and ROSE CHARLES DE MILLS. When planting allow room for the flower heads to mingle without touching and be careful near roses not to get manure around the alliums. SCHUBERTII a similar height to Cristophii bears huge 30cm (1') globes in early summer but the pale purple flowers are less dense being individually of different lengths; this gives the effect of an exploding aerial firework which is notably elegant. GIGANTEUM has a 10cm (4") lilac-pink starburst in summer but atop an impressive 1.5-2m (5-6') stem. CAERULEUM 60cm (24") high bears a 2.5cm (1") ball of star-shaped bright blue flowers in early summer. Alliums will increase through production of little bulblets adjacent to the main bulb.

Japanese ANEMONE - elegant performers in the late summer/early autumn mixed border. Make sure you choose the right spot as this is a plant that takes time to establish and is best left undisturbed after planting. Moist well-drained soil in sun or partial shade is ideal. Flowers are similar to clematis so these anemones could be incorporated within the vicinity of COTINUS, CLEMATIS and ROSES. The stalked flowers radiate from the top of tall, silky branched stems among dark green sharply-toothed leaves with hairy undersides. Recommended are A. HUPEHENSIS HADSPEN ABUNDANCE with deep pink flowers paling around the margins, 75cm (2½') high. A. x HYBRIDA HONORINE JOBERT has white flowers tinged pink on the back with golden-yellow stamens while MAX VOGEL bears light pink blooms that pale in maturity.

ANTHEMIS TINCTORIA E.C. BUXTON - daisy-like flowers in primrose-yellow borne throughout the summer on branching stems 45-70cm (18-28") high above mid-green ferny foliage downy-grey underneath. A. TINCTORIA GRALLAGH GOLD has golden-yellow flowers. A. SUSANNA MITCHELL provides a plethora of soft lemon flowers from May until November. Well-drained soil ideally with some horticultural grit added in full sun. Remove faded blooms regularly to prolong flowering. Going into autumn cut back hard to encourage the plant to make strong growth at the base which will remain evergreen through winter while protecting the plant against cold and dampness. If during summer the plant flops away from the centre reduce it by ½ and it will soon regain a bushy shape and make flowers. Good in pots.

AQUILEGIA - the columbines are firm favourites of traditional English gardens. They produce a lot of seed and the self-sets mingle naturalistically through the borders during late spring/early summer. They are easily raised from seed and there are many colours and forms to choose from. Well-drained soil in sun or partial shade will suffice. McKANA HYBRIDS will give a range of colours including lemon, pastel pink, blue and red. The flowers are bell-shaped with a cap of pointed petals which extend rearwards into long thin spiky tubes; carried on slender branched stems above rings of glaucous leaves. Up to 75cm (30") high. A. VULGARIS has flowers reminiscent of 'granny's bonnets' in shades of deep blue, purple, mauve, pink and white. 90cm (36") high.

ASTILBE - these contribute graceful plumes of flowers to the border and are especially suitable for organically enriched moist soil in full sun. Partial shade can be used if your soil is free-draining but always keep well watered and mulched. Very attractive in springtime when their emerging foliage is a striking red; particularly vibrant in the red flowered varieties. STRAUSSENFEDER which needs plenty of moisture to succeed has ferny foliage which is bronze tinted when young and dramatic sprays of deep pink flowers late summer/early autumn. 90cm (36") high. FANAL has dark green foliage with sprays of dark crimson flowers in early summer. 60cm (24") high. For drier soils PROFESSOR VAN DER WIEDEN tall at 1.2m (4') will give arching plumes of white flowers over mid-green foliage during midsummer. Particularly delicate is SPRITE with a tracery of shell-pink flowers above mid-green leaves in summer. 50cm (20") high. VENUS at 1m (3') high is noted for tapering spikes of soft silvery-pink flowers over bright green foliage in early summer. All flowerheads fade to shades of brown but keep their shape and can be left to catch the winter sunshine.

ASTRANTIA - delightful starry pincushion flowerheads surrounded by a ruff of tiny papery coloured leaves known as bracts borne in sprays on wiry stems from June to August. Colours include white, pink and ruby-red. Although they do well in a sunny spot dappled shade is preferred along with a moist soil with organic enrichment. Remove faded flowers to stimulate further blooms. When clumps become woody and less vigorous dig them up during dormancy and remove pieces around 5cm (2") across with little dormant growth buds and replant, discarding the remnants. A. MAJOR has green veined (sometimes shaded pink) bracts surrounding flowers which can be greeny-white, pink or purple-red. 30-90cm (12-36") high. Variety MAJOR SUNNINGDALE VARIEGATED has light green foliage irregularly edged cream and yellow which pales with age and greeny-white flowers with pink tinted bracts. 90cm (3') high. Fresh variegated leaves can be encouraged by removing fading foliage. Remember that variegation in any plant is due to a lack of chlorophyll in the non-green parts of the leaves making photosynthesis less efficient. With fewer energy-giving sugars produced growth will not be as vigorous so to compensate plant in a sunnier position. Attractive with pink ROSES. A. MAJOR HADSPEN BLOOD has wine-red bracts and flowers above red-tinged green leaves. A. MAJOR RUBY WEDDING is a lighter red. 90cm (3') high. MAJOR INVOLUCRATA SHAGGY bears large white flowers tinted green and pink with long white crimped green-tipped bracts with mid-pink undersides. 90cm (3') high. A. MAXIMA holds deep pink flowers dusted with pollen above starry paler pink bracts with emerald-green undersides early to midsummer. 60cm (24") high. Combine with feathery pink ASTILBE SPRITE and ROSA GLAUCA with its weathered copper foliage and pink flowers. A. MAJOR ROMA has clear rich pink flowers above silvery-pink bracts which acquire a greeny tinge with age. The unique structure of astrantias and their colours make them symbiotic partners for ACONITUM, ESCALLONIA and CLEMATIS PURPUREA PLENA ELEGANS.

CAMPANULA - although varying in form the flowers are mostly bell-shaped and range in colour from deep blue through the shades of blue into lilac and finally pure white. Plant in well-drained soil in sun or dappled shade. Will appreciate a scattering of Blood, Fish and Bone in spring or if you can get spent mushroom compost a mulch around (but not over). This contains lime which campanulas like but it pays to check if any of your plants are averse to lime before using mushroom compost as a general mulch. When the plants begin to lose vigour lift them and replant the healthy growths. Many campanulas have narrow leaves producing a 'see-through' effect which makes them ideal for the mixed border. It is worth noting that plants with narrow leaves tolerate dryness for longer; the smaller the surface area of the foliage the less water vapour is released keeping more moisture in reserve for the plant. C. PERSICIFOLIA has large lilac bells on slender stems 90cm (3') high early to midsummer. C. PERSICIFOLIA TELHAM BEAUTY has light blue bell-shaped flowers reaching the same height. C. PERSICIFOLIA ALBA has pure white bells and makes the same height. C. PERSICIFOLIA CHETTLE CHARM bears lilac-white bells 75cm (2½') high and blends well with pure white campanulas. C. PERSICIFOLIA MOERHEIMII has pure white flowers which resemble little cups and saucers. 90cm (3') high. C. PERSICIFOLIA ALBA CORONATA has white bell-shaped flowers but with an outer ring of petals which catch the light giving it extra radiance especially in dappled shade. 75cm (2½') high. C. PUNCTATA reaches 30cm (1') with dangling tubular bell-shaped flowers in the colour of crushed strawberry with a hint of white. Does well in sandy soil and in pots. C. GLOMERATA CAROLINE carries clusters of bell-shaped flowers in a soft pale mauve on upright stems throughout summer 45cm (18") high. With all campanulas remove flowers as they finish on the stem and when the stem itself is spent cut it off at the base to encourage new shoots. Left alone these plants will seed and self-sets will appear - even in the cracks of paving. In exposed areas a thin cane will prevent the stems from flopping. Their pastel shades and light elegance mingle well with ROSES e.g. blue campanulas with bold pink ZÉPHIRINE DROUHIN, ASTRANTIA, yellow AQUILEGIA and ANTHEMIS E.C. BUXTON. White campanulas mix effectively with pink flowers or plants showing yellow or gold such as ACHILLEA CORONATION GOLD with its ferny silvery-grey leaves.

CHAPTER ELEVEN
'PERENNIALS - SEASONED PERFORMERS YEAR AFTER YEAR'
TIM'S CHOICE PART 2

CONVALLARIA - known universally as LILY-OF-THE-VALLEY these beautifully scented little flowers are worth planting in a damp semi-shady part of the border for an enchanting late spring display. They will benefit from some organic matter incorporated in the soil. Left undisturbed they will increase year by year by means of an underground stem called a RHIZOME which produces buds and eventually new plants. Self-seeding also occurs. C. MAJALIS has arching stems 23cm (9") high bearing several small pure white waxy scented flowers like tiny ornate lampshades. Variety ROSEA has pale mauvish pink flowers. A mulch of bark chippings from the garden centre will highlight the flowers.

COREOPSIS - sunny yellow daisy-like flowers with ferny foliage on upright stems from mid to late summer. For full sun or partial shade in well-drained soil. Prolong flowering by removing spent flowers. As yellow reflects light these flowers are useful as radiant highlights within the mixed border and for illuminating shade. C. GRANDIFLORA BADENGOLD has deep yellow flowers with orangey centres and serrated edges to the petals 90cm (36") high. C. VERTICILLATA MOONBEAM bears pale yellow starry flowers on bronzy stems 45cm (18") high.

COSMOS ATROSANGUINEUS - known as the 'CHOCOLATE COSMOS' because its saucer-shaped velvety deep maroon flowers have a chocolate scent. Plant in moist well-drained soil in full sun in reach of inquiring noses! The 60cm (2') stems are reddish-brown with deep green leaves. Remove faded flowers to prolong flowering from midsummer to autumn. Interestingly this is a TUBEROUS perennial. When you plant it you will notice that within the root system are several carrot-like organs. Called tubers these store food and moisture for the plant while their 'eyes' or buds will form roots and shoots which will develop into flowering stems and below ground replacement and additional tubers for the following season. During dormancy these are susceptible to damage from frost and in cold damp conditions fungal attack. In well-drained soil in mild areas a deep dry mulch could keep the plant from harm. To be on the safe side though lift the tubers with a fork mid-autumn being careful not to spear any and gently brush off the soil. Cut the stems down to 15cm (6") turning the plant upside down under cover so surplus water can drain from the stems. Check the tubers for damage or disease removing any with a clean sharp knife and dusting with a fungicide available from garden centres. Place in a box of slightly moist peat in a frost-free place over winter checking occasionally for any disease. When the probability of frost has passed and the tubers have made shoots 2cm (1") long replant in the border 12cm (5") deep. Associate with silver or grey- leaved plants for good effect.

CROCOSMIA - bonfire colours mid to late summer in moist well-drained soil in sun or partial shade. Apply a deep dry mulch in autumn as insurance against the CORMS rotting. A corm functions in much the same way as a tuber producing replacement and additional corms. When the plants have increased in size they should be lifted in spring and new healthy growth replanted 8-10cm (3-4") deep with the remnants discarded. C. EMILY McKENZIE has downward-facing branched spikes of bright orange flowers with a brown marking inside each petal on wiry stems 60cm (24") high with slender mid-green leaves. C. LUCIFER reaches 90cm (3') with a profusion of trumpet-shaped upward-facing flaming red flowers on arching spikes. Effective against ACHILLEA CORONATION GOLD. C. SOLFATARE has sprays of small apricot-yellow flowers on arching branched stems with bronze-tinted leaves during midsummer 60-70cm (24-28") high. C. GOLDEN FLEECE bears in late summer slightly arching spikes of lemon-yellow flowers 60-75cm (24-30") high. C. MASONIORUM has upward-facing vermilion trumpets on arching spikes around 1.2m (4') high which makes it a good plant for the back of the border or against a wall. The foliage of crocosmia can appear almost translucent when backlit by the sun giving them a further dimension.

CYCLAMEN :- COUM and HEDERIFOLIUM - both tuberous perennials requiring organically enriched well-drained soil in partial shade. Dig in some horticultural grit to improve drainage if necessary. As the leaves wither apply an organic mulch ideally made with fallen leaves. C. coum bears flowers from January to late March in shades of white, pink and carmine all with a dark carmine mark in the centre. The leaves are rounded and range from shiny deep green patterned with grey to deep green marbled silver often with a dull red underneath. If you can, buy plants in bloom so you can see the colour and ensure the corms are 5cm (2") below soil level at planting. 5-8cm (2-3") high. C. hederifolium produces flowers; sometimes scented, in white or shades of pink with deep maroon marks in the centres mid to late autumn in advance of the foliage. Plant as C. coum. This plant is noted for its seedheads; following pollination the stems coil up spring-like and head for the ground where the seedheads eventually split releasing the seeds. These have a sugary coating which encourages ants who will move the seeds over quite a wide area ensuring an expanding carpet in following seasons. 10-13cm (4-5") high. The leaves emerge during September in shapes from broad shields to tapering arrowheads and hearts. Mid to dark green with an array of marbled silver patterning. They will become an enhancement for the garden through winter into spring. Both these varieties of cyclamen are ideal for planting underneath trees and shrubs and would look especially effective with BIRCH, VIBURNUM x BODNANTENSE DAWN with its complimentary sugar-pink flowers and CHAENOMELES UMBILICATA with dark pink flowers.

DAHLIA - tuberous perennials with the same basics for cultivation as Cosmos Atrosanguineus. However for more flowering stems and manageable height the growing tip of each stem can be removed when two pairs of leaves have developed (around April). When this has stimulated the secondary buds into making stems themselves with two pairs of leaves these too can have their growing tips removed (around May).

ANNEX: 'TOOL UP'.

Time to get a GARDEN KNIFE for tasks such as removing growing tips cleanly and eventually increasing plants by taking cuttings. Good ironmongers or garden centres will have several all capable of tackling these tasks. I would recommend a GRAFTING KNIFE with a forged carbon steel blade which folds back into a polished walnut handle. BE CAREFUL - it is RAZOR-SHARP and should be kept that way by using your ceramic file and wiping with an oily rag from time to time. As always buy the best you can afford.

Dahlias should be planted in the border when the probability of frost is over 12cm (5") deep. A cane will be needed to tie the plant to as it grows so put one in before planting to avoid spearing a tuber! These plants appreciate plenty of organic matter in the soil and an application of Blood, Fish and Bone would be appropriate. Take precautions against slugs too. BISHOP OF LLANDAFF is an old time favourite - black-red foliage setting off fiery red blooms with bright yellow anthers (the tip of the stamen containing pollen). 1.1m (3½') high. DAVID HOWARD has bronze foliage and soft orange flowers. Both would look well with CROCOSMIAS EMILY McKENZIE and LUCIFER, ACHILLEA CORONATION GOLD, LAVENDER, COTINUS, hip-bearing ROSES e.g. MOYESII GERANIUM and ACONITUM. Silver-leaved plants provide a good contrast for the 'Bishop' and MURDOCH with cherry-red flowers suffused green at the centre. FASCINATION is just 60cm (24") high with dark bronze foliage and vivid purplish-pink blooms blending well with JAPANESE ANEMONES and AGAPANTHUS. CLAIR DE LUNE flowers have an outer ring of pale yellow petals, a cream inner ring and deep yellow anthers in the centre. 1.1m (3½') high. GLORIE VAN HEEMSTEDE has buttercup-yellow flowers on stems 1.3m (4½') high; especially dramatic in late afternoon sunshine and with CROCOSMIA SOLFATARE. Enjoy Dahlias from midsummer to late autumn depending on the first frost.

DICENTRA - known as 'Bleeding Heart' due to its dangling heart-shaped flowers. SPECTABLIS has pale green ferny leaves and arching maroon-tinted stems bearing hearts rose-pink on the outside and white inside with a long teardrop. 75cm (2½') tall performing from late spring into early summer. The slightest breeze will cause the hearts to delightfully quiver. Another common name is 'lady in the bathtub' - look inside the flower using your imagination to see why! SPECTABLIS ALBA has pure white hearts and flowers into midsummer. Plant in well-drained moisture retentive soil ideally in partial shade and feed in February with Blood, Fish and Bone to maintain vigour.

DIERAMA PULCHERRIMUM - often referred to as 'Angel's Fishing Rod' with its 1 1.5m (3-5') graceful arching stems bearing pendular deep-pink bells above grass-like foliage during midsummer. This habit allows for effective underplanting. Especially attractive when wafting in a breeze. Plant in moist well-drained organically enriched soil in sun with your fingers crossed as Dierama (another corm) is not the easiest perennial to establish but well worth trying.

DIGITALIS (FOXGLOVE) - the elegant thrusting spires are a must for the mixed border combining very effectively with ROSES, CAMPANULAS, ASTRANTIAS, HOLLYHOCKS and ALLIUMS. Their vividly striking colours and markings especially popular with bees also make foxgloves ideal for an attractive and impressive group planting. Perform from late May to late July. Grow in soil organically enriched and reasonably moisture retentive in partial shade if possible. They produce an enormous amount of seed so it is cheap to buy from garden centres and really easy to grow into plants which will flower in their second year. (Raising plants from seed is explained in the chapter on annuals). Once you have foxgloves self-set plants should ensure them being around for many years. As the flower spike comes to the end of its display cut it off; shaking out seed on to the border for self-sets or on to a newspaper to save for you-sows. The plant will produce some new flowering sideshoots. You can of course source plants from the usual places. Recommended are PURPUREA EXCELSIOR HYBRIDS - 120-150cm (48-60") - tubular bells in creamy-yellow, white, purple and pink with interior mottling. PURPUREA APRICOT with a brown mottling and the same height mixes well with yellow flowers. PURPUREA FOXY HYBRIDS has flowers of carmine-red, pink, creamy-yellow, white and a dark mottled maroon. Just 90cm (36") this is ideal for smaller spaces and windy positions. PURPUREA ALBA WHITE is particularly striking being driven-snow white without markings. 120cm (48").

ECHINACEA - impressive and tall each plant bearing several strong stems with large daisy-like flowers; petals inclined downwards and a prominent gingery cone at the centre. Hence the common name of 'Coneflower'. Will thrive in well-drained organically enriched soil in full sun or partial shade. Take precautions to avoid slugs and snails damaging new growth in spring and staking may be required in exposed positions. Noteworthy for strong colour and distinct shape mid to late summer they also have a honey scent which brings in bees and butterflies while the seedheads provide food for birds. E. PURPUREA MAGNUS has wide flat reddish-pink flowers whose composition gives them a swirling effect with distinct luminous orange cones on stems 80-120cm (2½ - 4') high. WHITE SWAN is the same height and has creamy-white flowers around a greenish-gingery cone. LEUCHSTERN has large rosy-pink flowers 80cm (32") high. AUGUST KÖNIGIN bears large pinky-mauve flowers 80-120cm (2½-4') high. CROCOSMIA LUCIFER looks good in the vicinity of ECHINACEA whose slender stems also combine well with those of ALLIUM.

ERIGERON KARVINSKIANUS PROFUSION - a bright self-seeding plant with pink or white yellow-centred daisy-like flowers which is useful for filling gaps in paving and walls.

ERYNGIUM - colour, texture, form and shape; eryngium has them all. E. GIGANTEUM is known as 'Miss Willmott's ghost' after this Edwardian gardener who amused herself secretly scattering this plant's seed whilst visiting gardens to surprise the owners the following season! This story proves it is easy to grow from seed and since it produces a lot you will always have fresh plants. The plant sends down a taproot (like a long carrot) so once it's in leave it as there is a good chance this will be damaged if transplanted. Happy in coastal regions and in dry well-drained even impoverished soil in full sun and out of winter wet. Erect stems 90cm (3') high with bristly steel-blue cones surrounded by prickly ruffs of papery silver-grey leaves from midsummer into autumn. E. ALPINUM has a soft blue cone with a more lacy ruff of grey-blue. Stems 60cm (2') high are blue to white and the leaves mid-green and heart shaped. These plants mix well with white flowered companions and also with COTINUS COGGYGRIA ROYAL PURPLE ideally clothed with a dusky red CLEMATIS such as MADAME EDOUARD ANDRÉ. Or in the vicinity of ROSE GRAHAM THOMAS with its deep yellow flowers and AGAPANTHUS BEN HOPE.

FOENICULUM VULGARE PURPUREUM - the bronze Fennel is invaluable for instilling a frothy softening effect on reds, oranges and yellows e.g. CROCOSMIAS LUCIFER AND SOLFATARE. Also CORNUS ALBA SIBIRICA. Or perhaps combining with DIERAMA PULCHERRIMUM. Large plumes of bronze-purple foliage give way to 180 cm (6') stems with clouds of fine bronze foliage with starbursts of mustard-yellow flowers. Again COTINUS COGGYGRIA ROYAL PURPLE is an effective associate. The seedheads keep their form which is ideal for cutting and spraying for flower arrangements but they will shed a large number of seeds resulting in many self-sets. Aniseed scented fennel is best planted in organically enriched moist well-drained soil in full sun. Do not transplant as this is a tap rooting plant.

GERANIUM - very useful plants for the mixed border having a variety of habits, flower colour and leaf form. They grow well in free-draining but moisture retentive soil in full sun or partial shade. Plants such as CAMPANULA with rather sparse stems will benefit from a geranium which can weave around while providing complimentary or contrasting colour. So will ROSES and CISTUS. In fact perennials such as geraniums will stop the fungal spores of diseases such as blackspot from splashing up from the soil on to the rose leaves. When flowering is over remove the spent flowers and foliage to the ground; fork around, water and feed with either Blood, Fish and Bone or an organic mulch. This will trigger young fresh foliage and more flowers. The following are recommended:- ANN FOLKARD; a good scrambler with 45cm (18") stems and a profusion of saucer-shaped violet flowers with black centres and veins from midsummer to mid-autumn. Leaves mature from yellow to soft green. G. x RIVERSLEAIANUM RUSSELL PRITCHARD produces deep magenta funnel-shaped flowers throughout summer. Up to 23cm (9") high with grey-green sharply-toothed leaves. Combines well with ALCHEMILLA MOLLIS. MAVIS SIMPSON has silvery-pink saucer-shaped blooms above soft green silver-edged leaves all summer. 15cm (6") high. JOHNSON'S BLUE bears saucer-shaped lavender-blue flowers 30-45cm (12-18") late spring into summer. G. PRATENSE MRS KENDAL CLARK has clear mauve-blue white veined flowers which are especially attractive in the evening. The mid-green leaves acquire a red tint by autumn. 90cm (3') high which makes it ideal for growing among some old shrub ROSES which will help support it while being enhanced. Late spring into summer. G. SANGUINEUM STRIATUM has pale pink flowers veined darker pink during summer. 23cm (9") high. G. SANGUINEUM ALBUM has saucer-shaped flowers of pure white throughout summer 30cm (12") high. G. OXONIANUM WARGRAVE PINK is a vigorous plant 60cm (24") high with deep pink flowers. CLARIDGE DRUCE is a strong grower 45cm (18") high with a long display of bright pink flowers veined magenta. Grey-green leaves. ENDRESSII bears a succession of bright pink funnel-shaped flowers with a silvery sheen from early summer to early autumn 45cm (18") above light green leaves. G. HIMALAYENSE GRAVETYE has large violet-blue flowers with white centres veined dark pink 30cm

(12") above frilly mid-green leaves. G. PSILOSTEMON bears a profusion of bowl-shaped magenta flowers with deep purple centres and veins from early to late summer. 60cm (2') plus above mid-green foliage which has crimson tints in spring and red in autumn. When plants become congested trim around with your spade or alternatively lift and replant the vigorous outer growths discarding the old woody bits.

GEUM - a plant for organically enriched well-drained soil in full sun. LADY STRATHEDEN is recommended growing to 45cm (18") high with striking buttercup-yellow flowers late spring through summer.

GYPSOPHILA PANICULATA BRISTOL FAIRY grows up to 90cm (3') high with slim airy stems bearing frothy sprays of small pure white bobble-like flowers during midsummer. Grow in full sun in deep (to accomodate its tap root) very well-drained soil. Add horticultural grit to increase draining. Effective with DIERAMA PULCHERRIMUM.

HELENIUM - every mixed border needs these for their glowing embers colours during late summer into autumn. Attractive to bees and other pollinators. Plant in moisture retentive well-drained soil in sun or partial shade with a mulch. When plants become congested lift in spring separating and replanting the vigorous outer shoots with a dressing of Blood, Fish and Bone. Discard the remainder. Remove spent flowers regularly and in exposed positions support with garden twine tied around three canes. MOERHEIM BEAUTY has orangey-red daisy-shaped flowers with a domed velvety brownish-gold centre. Growing to 90cm (3') the blooms mature to burnt orange. H. PUMILUM MAGNIFICUM bears golden-yellow flowers with yellow-brown centres and is the same height. H. WYNDLEY has yellow flowers that appear 'colourwashed' with deep orange and orangey-brown centres. Similar height the flowers mature to brick-red. SAHIN'S EARLY FLOWERER has a particularly long season with shimmering mahogany-orange flowers. Heleniums meld well with CROCOSMIAS EMILY McKENZIE and LUCIFER, DAHLIAS BISHOP OF LLANDAFF and DAVID HOWARD, FOENICULUM VULGARE PURPUREUM, AGAPANTHUS, ACONITUM and ACHILLEA CORONATION GOLD. All harmonious in colour but so contrasting in flower, shape and form.

HELIANTHUS - known as the 'Perennial Sunflower' these plants will thrive in well-drained moisture retentive soil in full sun. To maintain vigour maintain as instructed for Heleniums. H. LEMON QUEEN reaches 1.5m (5½') with starry pale yellow flowers and light green foliage. H. ATRORUBENS MONARCH a similar height has bright yellow shaggy flowers with brown centres which in time become dusted with yellow pollen. Carried on slender branched stems. Slightly lower at 1.2m (4') is H. x MULTIFLORUS TRIOMPHE DE GAND with golden-yellow daisy-like flowers. All add colourful height to the mixed border from late summer into autumn and blend well with ECHINACEA, the darker blue AGAPANTHUS, HELENIUMS and BUDDLEJA.

HELIOPSIS - worth including with HELENIUM and HELIANTHUS is SOMMERSONNE bearing golden yellow slightly orangey flowers with brownish-yellow centres. 90cm (36") high.

HELLEBORUS - ideal for planting under the deciduous trees and shrubs where they will appreciate light in winter/early spring and shade in summer. Otherwise a partially or dappled shaded site with cool, moist well-drained soil with plenty of organic enrichment. H. x HYBRIDUS come in a range of colours which can be symbiotically combined with trees such as BIRCH and many of the winter into spring flowering shrubs. From mid-winter to mid-spring stout branching stems up to 45cm (18") high bear clusters of saucer-shaped flowers above leathery mid to dark green leaves. Because the colours include white, purple, yellow, green and pink it is a good idea to choose your hellebores while they are in flower so you know what you are getting. If you have chosen some winter into spring shrubs from chapter seven you can see which hellebores will look striking with them - either complimentary or contrasting. For example VIBURNUM x BODNANTENSE DAWN with pink helleborus, HAMAMELIS with yellow, CORNUS ALBA SIBIRICA with white etc. White and pastel coloured hellebores are especially attractive when they catch the low winter light. Many of the flowers have delicate maroon speckles inside which can give a further dimension when underplanting shrubs. H. BALLARDIAE DECEMBER DAWN 35cm (14") high has saucer-shaped white flowers flushed pink which becomes purplish with age. A good companion for VIBURNUM x BODNANTENSE DAWN along with CYCLAMEN COUM. Hellebores around the base of CHAENOMELES is another pleasing combination. H. CYCLOPHYLLUS bears clusters of pendent saucer-shaped pale green scented flowers. 40cm (16") high. H. NIGER (known as the 'CHRISTMAS ROSE') POTTER'S WHEEL has delightful bowl-shaped pure white flowers with green centres and yellow stamens. Around 30cm (12") high. For appearance and to prevent fungal disease taking hold remove ageing leaves when new ones come and use bark chippings as a mulch to protect the flowers from being splashed with soil.

HEUCHERA - several recommendations here:- BRESSINGHAM BRONZE not surprisingly with dark bronze evergreen leaves and upright stems bearing creamy-white bell-shaped flowers. STRAWBERRY SWIRL with bright green ruffled leaves patterned with silver and delicate flowers the colour of strawberry ice-cream. CHOCOLATE RUFFLES with veined mahogany-red burnished bronze frilly heart-shaped leaves and red stems carrying tiny creamy flowers. H. MICRANTHA variety DIVERSIFOLIA PALACE PURPLE has bronzey purple-red leaves and greenish-white tubular flowers with red anthers followed by pink seedheads. PLUM PUDDIN has glossy silky plum-coloured leaves and silvery undertones. REGINA has reddish-purple scalloped leaves with silvering between the veins and pink flowers. MINT FROST has pale minty-green foliage with aluminium undertones. Heuchera's flower spikes grow from around 30cm (12") to 45cm (18") during early to mid-summer but it is for their foliage that they are renowned adding value and creating impact when combined with yellows, reds, maroons, silvers, whites and blues throughout the year. For example dark silver veined heucheras around LAVENDER and ASTRANTIAS RUBY WEDDING and HADSPEN BLOOD. And the lovely new maroon growth of ROSES is accentuated when heucheras are integrated. Try them around FOENICULUM VULGARE PURPUREUM too. Heucheras do best in sun (looking especially radiant when backlit) but partial shade is acceptable. Moisture retentive but well-drained soil will enable the plants to make good clumps. Remove any scruffy leaves as new ones emerge and after about three years you will notice that the plant has become unwieldy with fresh growth at the top of bare stems. To return to lush clumps lift the plant either in spring or late summer cutting off the healthy growth with about 5cm (2") of the stem discarding the rest. Replant in organically enriched soil (they like spent mushroom compost) with the lower leaves just above the surface where they will soon send out new roots.

HOSTA - their leaves are striking - depending on variety green, yellow, grey-blue or variegated shaped like discs, eggs, lances or hearts. Plus erect stems with tubular or bell-shaped flowers usually white or in shades of mauve. On the face of it indispensable plants for the mixed border when grouping plants for unity and contrast. However slugs and snails can rapidly destroy all that is effective with hostas reducing the foliage to unsightly tatters. If your garden has frogs, hedgehogs and thrushes then the problem will be largely eaten. Otherwise see what is available for discouraging or killing slugs and snails. They are a major problem in gardens especially in the vicinity of any new growth and progress is being made in finding solutions which are in harmony with the natural system of the garden. It is good practice to keep ones eyes open for slugs and snails; from late autumn into spring snails cluster together in dormancy where it is dry - within evergreens, behind flower pots, around stones and pieces of wood. Caught napping they can be gathered and ejected! Ideal conditions for hostas are moist but well-drained soil out of the wind. Partial shade is best but full shade will do although there will be fewer flowers. Yellow-leaved varieties will have better colour if planted within reach of the morning sun. In spring mulch with organic material. Hostas look particularly effective when planted in the dappled shade of white stemmed BIRCHES. ROSES especially those with bluey-grey leaves blend well with hostas of the same hue. Hostas with lime-green leaves make an attractive picture with the purple flowered ALLIUMS also giving interest at ground level where allium foliage is somewhat scruffy. Purple DIGITALIS will benefit from hostas with unifying or contrasting foliage at their base. Recommended are :- H. ANTIOCH - oval arching matt dark green leaves with marginal variations of grey-green and creamy-yellow maturing to white, bluey-mauve flowers 50cm (20") high. H. BIRCHWOOD PARKY'S GOLD - heart-shaped matt yellow-green leaves maturing to deep yellow, pale mauve flowers 35-40cm (14-16") high. H. BLUE BLUSH - lance-shaped glaucous blue-green leaves, bluey-mauve flowers 20cm (8") high. H. GOLD STANDARD - oval greeny yellow leaves maturing yellow then cream with dark green edgings, bluey-mauve flowers 1.1m (3½') high. H. HADSPEN BLUE - heart-shaped robust grey-blue leaves, grey-mauve flowers 25cm (10") high. H. MOONLIGHT - oval slightly dished lime-green foliage maturing to yellow edged in white, bluey-mauve flowers 65cm (26") high. All flower midsummer. In springtime hostas are particularly attractive as the new leaves unfurl.

INULA - bees and butterflies flock to these cheerful daisy flowers during mid to late summer and they look attractive with HELENIUMS, HELIANTHUS and COREOPSIS. Plant in moisture retentive well-drained soil. I. HOOKERI has light green foliage which along with its stems and buds are furry to touch. The flowers are pale yellow with brownish-yellow centres and finely petalled. Does best in partial shade. 60-75cm (24-30") high.

LAMIUM - MACULATUM BEACON SILVER is worth including mainly for its attractive silver leaves which are edged green. Up to 15cm (6") high with deep pink hooded flowers. Will symbiotically combine with HOSTA ANTIOCH and HEUCHERA MICRANTHA v. DIVERSIFOLIA PALACE PURPLE. Grow in moist well-drained soil in full or partial shade which will be diminished by its ability to reflect light.

LEUCANTHEMUM - daisy-like flowers in driven-snow white from early summer to early autumn. Radiant in the evening especially in moonlight and on dull days. Attractive in the company of ASTRANTIA and DAHLIAS. Also HELENIUMS, COREOPSIS and HELIANTHUS whose yellow shades will compliment the yellow centres of the following:- L. x SUPERBUM PHYLLIS SMITH - with shaggy flowers and T.E. KILLIN whose daisy-type outer petals give way to short tufted petals near the centre. 90cm (3') in height on erect stems with deep green serrated leaves. Moist well-drained soil in sun or partial shade. May need staking.

CHAPTER TWELVE
'PERENNIALS - SEASONED PERFORMERS YEAR AFTER YEAR'
TIM'S CHOICE PART 3

LILIUM - there are many varieties of colourful fragrant LILIES but for the mixed border I am recommending just two; L. CANDIDUM the MADONNA LILY and L. REGALE the REGAL LILY. Be aware that the pollen can be harmful to CATS if it gets on their fur and is licked off. The best time to buy is in spring, lilies are BULBS which will be explained in a later chapter. Choose lily bulbs that are plump and firm around the base; not shrivelled or showing any signs of mould. Before planting incorporate plenty of organic matter plus horticultural grit to improve drainage. The Madonna Lily will need to sit on a little heap of grit to prevent rotting with its nose just below the soil surface. The Regal Lily though requires planting still on a heap of grit but at a depth of around 3x the height of the bulb. This is a stem-rooting lily meaning that the bulb not only makes roots from underneath but also from the stem above the bulb until it reaches the light. This gives extra support for the plant which can reach between 0.6 and 2m (2-6') high. With a similar height for the Madonna Lily staking would be wise. Allow space of around 3x the diameter of the bulb between them. Both varieties benefit from being in the company of other plants as these will give shade to the soil surface giving the lilies a cool root run while allowing their flowers to be in full sun. Watch out for slugs and snails and if necessary water at the base of the plant. In midsummer the Madonna Lily produces clusters of extremely sweetly scented trumpet-shaped pure white flowers with yellow bases and anthers 5-8cm (2-3") long. During the winter some leaves will remain at the base to continue maintaining the plant. The Regal Lily bears very fragrant trumpet-shaped white flowers streaked purple on the outsides with yellow centres and gold anthers 12-15cm (5-6") long. The stems are attractive too being grey-green with a purple tinge and shiny deep green leaves. Variety ALBUM has pure white flowers but with orange anthers. Both plants are particularly beautiful in the evening and by moonlight so try and position the lilies near to windows, doors and seats and where it is sheltered - not just to protect the flowers but here the calmer air will hold the scent for longer. On a general note scent is strengthened by hot weather and varies through the day in quality and intensity as the flower matures. A good contrast for these lilies would be DAHLIA BISHOP OF LLANDAFF. They would also meld well with CAMPANULAS, pale HOLLYHOCKS, LEUCANTHEMUM, pastel coloured ROSES, FOXGLOVES, HONEYSUCKLE and PHILADELPHUS SYBILLE.

LOBELIA CARDINALIS - although not the easiest of plants to keep it is worth trying for its vivid scarlet flowers clustered on dark red stems with glossy bronzey bright green leaves. Summer to early autumn. So useful for combining with DAHLIA BISHOP OF LLANDAFF, CROCOSMIA LUCIFER and COTINUS. 90cm (36") high. Plant in moisture retentive well-drained soil in sun or partial shade. In autumn feed with Blood, Fish and Bone to build the plant up for the winter making sure all stems have been cut back so that they cannot rot into the crown and to stimulate the production of new crowns. Slugs and snails can be a problem on early growth so take precautions.

LYCHNIS CORONARIA - a perennial which regenerates itself by self-sets enabling you to always have vigorous plants. Overwinters as an evergreen rosette of soft grey-green leaves with silver hairs. Upright branched stems of the same hue 75cm (2½') high bear clusters of flat rich carmine pink flowers in summer. Plant in very well-drained soil in sun or partial shade. Its random seeding will enable it to weave naturally around ROSES; those with dark green leaves accentuating the shape, form and texture of the lychnis while the flowers could contrast or compliment. HEUCHERAS and GERANIUMS such as MAVIS SIMPSON would add to the picture.

LYSIMACHIA CILIATA FIRECRACKER is worth having because of its chocolate-brown foliage and yellow starry flowers on erect stems in summer. Tall at 120cm (4') it needs moisture retentive well-drained soil in sun or partial shade and may need staking. Very attractive in spring when the foliage emerges bronze. Any plants with yellow flowers would look well in its company and for contrast FOENICULUM VULGARE PURPUREUM especially.

LYTHRUM - grow in moisture retentive soil in full sun. L. SALICARIA BLUSH has 90cm (3') spires of blush-pink star-shaped flowers from midsummer to early autumn. L. VIRGATUM THE ROCKET at 80cm (32") produces deep pink columns. A nice accompaniment for ECHINACEA.

MALVA - the musk mallow M. MOSCHATA is a bushy plant with slightly musk-scented mid-green leaves reaching up to 90cm (36") high. Throughout the summer into early autumn it bears clusters of saucer-shaped pale pink flowers. Variety ALBA has pure white flowers slightly veined with green. A good companion for ERYNGIUM and ASTRANTIA MAJOR. Requires moisture retentive well-drained soil in sun or partial shade.

MECONOPSIS CAMBRICA - the WELSH POPPY blooming from mid-spring to mid-autumn with delightful shallow cup-shaped lemon-yellow to orange flowers. On slender stalks around 30cm (1') high borne on branched stems with pale to bluish-green leaves. Grow in moisture retentive well-drained soil in full to partial shade into sun. Remove spent blooms to ensure a succession of flowers but leave a few to seed around in an attractive natural way which in time will include cracks in walls and paving. Because of its tap-root do not try to dig up and replant. Radiant at dusk and when backlit by the sun especially in a breeze.

OENOTHERA - speciosa ROSEA is a ground covering plant growing to 30cm (12"). Likes full sun in well-drained soil and is tap-rooted. From mid-afternoon from early summer to early autumn on arching stems open large saucer-shaped exquisitely scented white flowers strongly suffused pink with deep pink veins and greeny-yellow centres. Interestingly this is pollinated by moths (whites and pastel shades being more visible to them although they rely mainly on scent to draw them to nectar) so the flowers are particularly enchanting as daylight fades. Will compliment ROSES of similar hues, white FOXGLOVES, CAMPANULAS, pale HOLLYHOCKS and HONEYSUCKLE.

PAPAVER ORIENTALE - although the flowering time is relatively short; late spring into early summer the sheer elegance and splendour of the flowers books them space in the mixed border. Plant in organically enriched well-drained soil in sun or partial shade and apply a dressing of Blood, Fish and Bone in early spring when growth starts from the overwintered clumps of roughly-textured mid-green leaves. The white bristled stems look sturdy but are inclined to flop so support them with garden twine tied around canes to keep them erect as they develop. Each stem produces a hairy bud and when you see the outer casing split to reveal the colour of the tightly-packed flower hang around because you are about to see something quite wonderful. The casing will suddenly ping off and the flower will gradually unfurl into a cup-shape with petals looking as if they are made from crepe paper. At the centre is a velvety seed pod surrounded by black stamens like eyelashes. When the flowers have finished remove the stems at ground level and the plant will produce a neat clump of fresh leaves around which later flowering plants can perform. Before the plants make real progress in spring they can be lifted and divided into individual fresh growths which can be replanted. Alternatively you can increase your plants by taking ROOT CUTTINGS in late autumn/early winter during dormancy. You can also try this technique with CAMPANULA, JAPANESE ANEMONE, DICENTRA and GYPSOPHILA. Lift the plant and wash the soil off the roots; cut some young vigorous roots below the crown with your grafting knife (don't take more than ⅓ of the root system and replant the crown straight away). As the cuttings will need enough food on board to survive and regenerate they should be pencil-thick 5cm (2") long. So you know the top from the bottom make a straight cut for the top and an angled cut for the bottom. Gently ease them into the compost in a pot (to ensure there are no air gaps around the root) with the top level with the compost surface. Top-dress with horticultural grit and water. Place on a warm windowsill keeping the compost moist. Hopefully the cuttings will be stimulated into making some shoots given every plant's aim to reproduce itself. When this happens transfer the little plants individually to 75mm (3") pots planting out when the roots have filled the pot. Recommended are ALLEGRO - bright orangey-red flowers with black markings at the base. CURLILOCKS - again orangey-red but fringed petals. TURKISH DELIGHT - pale pink flowers. These three are particularly robust in wet weather. BLACK AND WHITE - large white ruffled flowers with a crimson-black mark at the base of each petal. Especially effective at dusk. CEDRIC MORRIS - large frilly pale pink flowers with maroon marks at each petal's base. KARINE - salmon-pink saucer-shaped flowers 60cm (2') high. MRS PERRY - slightly deeper salmon-pink with black marks at the base of each petal. PERRY'S WHITE - not surprisingly pure white but with maroon-purple marks at each petal's base. PATTY'S PLUM - large ruffled flowers of dusky plum-purple which look attractive in the company of ASTRANTIAS RUBY WEDDING and

HADSPEN BLOOD. PICOTEE - creased petals of white suffused orange. TURKENLOUIS - unless stated all the poppies here are around 90cm (3') high but this is slightly taller at 105cm (3½'). Large frilly red-hot blooms with black marks on each petal and a black centre. BEAUTY OF LIVERMERE - really tall at 120cm (4') with large scarlet flowers with a black mark at each petal's base.

PHLOX PANICULATA - should be included in every flower garden for their large, shapely heads of vibrantly coloured flowers combined with a powerful scent. Ideal for planting near PAPAVER ORIENTALE and AQUILEGIA where they can develop during these plants 'closed season'. They also combine well with ROSES. Grow in organically enriched moisture retentive but well-drained soil in sun although partial shade will suffice. Remove spikes as they finish in the hope of stimulating new ones and in autumn mulch with organic matter. Will flower from summer to early/mid-autumn. Recommended are:- AMETHYST with rose-pink flowers. BALMORAL with deep pink flowers. BRIGHT EYES bearing pale pink flowers with deep pink centres. EUROPE with white flowers and carmine centres. EVA CULLUM with bright pink flowers. EVENTIDE with lavender-blue flowers - one for partial shade. SANDRINGHAM with pale pink flowers and deeper pink centres. All 90cm (36") high. Slightly lower is FUJIYAMA at 75cm (30") with pure white flowers. White and pale pink phlox blend well with DAHLIAS of similar hues, tall slender-stemmed blue AGAPANTHUS and also look attractive at twilight with white CAMPANULA. Same height is MOTHER OF PEARL with rounded white flowers tinged pink - very attractive in the company of plants with silver, grey and pastel hues, LYTHRUM for example.

PIMPINELLA - worthy for its flower structure and shape so giving good contrast when used in the mixed border. Erect to 1.2m (4') with pretty ferny mid-green leaves and clusters of tiny star like flowers like little umbrellas in white, greenish white (P MAJOR) and deep/pale pink (P. MAJOR ROSEA). Very effective at twilight. From spring into midsummer. Grow in organically enriched well-drained moisture retentive soil in full sun or partial shade. Watch out for SLUGS and SNAILS - the young growth of this plant and many others can be a ready meal for them!

POLEMONIUM - known as 'Jacob's Ladder' and a cottage garden

favourite. The leaves are mid-green and look like a ladder. Plant in organically enriched moisture retentive soil but well-drained with the help of some horticultural grit, in full sun or partial shade. Recommended are;- P. CAERULEUM growing between 30-90cm (12-36") high and bearing small clusters of lavender-blue bell-shaped flowers on erect branched stems during early to midsummer. P. LAMBROOK MAUVE reaches 45cm (18") in height with branched stalks carrying loose bunches of funnel-shaped lilac-blue flowers from mid-spring into early summer. Both meld well with ROSES and HOLLYHOCKS. .

PRIMULA VULGARIS - the sight of the enchantingly beautiful pale lemon flowers of the common PRIMROSE are so welcome in the garden throughout spring. Up to 15cm (6") high they appreciate organically enriched well-drained but moisture retentive soil in a spot which will receive partial shade in summer. After flowering mulch with some organic matter and apply some Blood, Fish and Bone. When the plants begin to look tired and woody lift and replant the fresh growths after trimming the roots to 10cm (4"). Best done in autumn. The plant forms a rosette of mid-green lance-shaped deeply-veined leaves which largely disappear during summer. ENSURE that you buy plants which have been raised in a nursery not nicked from the countryside.

PULMONARIA - spring flowerers and (since they like the same conditions) suitable for planting in the company of HELLEBORES and PRIMROSES. The varieties whose leaves have silvery markings combine well with those of CYCLAMEN HEDERIFOLIUM, also LAMIUM. Underplanting any of the spring flowering SHRUBS with pulmonarias will not only create a lovely spring display but also give the pulmonarias necessary partial shade in summer. The colours of pulmonaria flowers blend especially well with those of other spring flowering shrubs and perennials. They appreciate organically enriched soil which is moisture retentive in summer. The base of a shady wall is a possibility. In winter remove older scruffy leaves to encourage new foliage and to enable the flowers to come through easily and to look nice. Mulch with organic matter. Remove faded flowers to encourage the making of new flowers and leaves. These early flowers are especially useful to bees. Recommended are :- P. ANGUSTIFOLIA BLUE ENSIGN with dark green pointed leaves and purple buds which open as violet-blue flowers held in clusters. P. ANGUSTIFOLIA LEWIS

PALMER bears rich blue funnel-shaped flowers after opening pink above lance-shaped hairy dark green leaves with greenish-white markings. P. LONGIFOLIA MAWSON'S BLUE has hairy dark green leaves below dark blue flowers. All 35cm (14") high. P. VALLARSAE MARGERY FISH has bright green leaves with silver markings and flowers which mature pink through mauve to violet. P. OFFICINALIS SISSINGHURST WHITE has silvery-white markings on its pale green leaves and small sprays of delicate pure white flowers opening as pale pink buds. 30cm (12") high. P. OFFICINALIS ROY DAVIDSON bears sprays of soft blue flowers above spotted leaves. P. RUBRA DAVID WARD has pale green leaves margined cream with clusters of coral-red flowers. All around 30cm (1') in height.

RANUNCULUS - R. ficaria the lesser celandine brings early spring colour to the edges of paving (and between the paving stones), under shrubs and around the other perennials in season. Moisture retentive organically enriched soil in full or partial shade is best although self-sets establish anywhere! A dressing of Blood, Fish and Bone during growth will be appreciated. After flowering the leaves die down so make sure you mark where they are! R. FICARIA ALBUS has dark bronze leaves and very pale yellow flowers which mature to white. R. AURANTIACUS has silvery leaves with bronze markings and coppery-orange flowers which have slightly darker backs. BRAZEN HUSSY makes glossy mahogany-coloured leaves with shining golden yellow flowers which are tinted bronze on their backs. All just 5cm (2") high. R. GRAMINEUS is for the border itself growing 30cm (12") high and liking moisture retentive well-drained soil in sun or partial shade. The leaves are grass-like and grey-green in colour. Late spring into early summer come bright yellow buttercup flowers (Ranunculus includes the common buttercup) borne on upright branched stems.

RUDBECKIA - more sunny daisy-shaped flowers for midsummer into early autumn. R. FULGIDA SULLIVANTII GOLDSTURM literally translates as 'goldstorm' with a prolific display of golden yellow flowers with blackish-brown conical centres on erect stems 60cm (24") high. Dark green leaves. Looks attractive with red and white DAHLIAS. R. HERBSTSONNE is very tall at 2m (6') so would be best at the back of the border. Golden yellow flowers with greeny conical centres which mature to yellowish-brown are borne on branched stems with glossy mid-green leaves.. The petals droop downwards. Rudbeckia does best in soil which remains moist during summer either in full sun or partial shade.

SAXIFRAGA x URBIUM - LONDON PRIDE; a tough little plant with flower spikes reaching 30cm (12") high during summer. These are slender branching stems with small star-shaped white flowers tinged pink. Like many such delicate flowers its beautiful intricacy is best appreciated through a HAND LENS. This is a spreading plant ideal for blurring the edges between paths and borders and forms mats of mid-green, leathery, serrated-edged spoon-shaped leaves. Well-drained moisture retentive soil is preferred in sun or partial shade but in reality poor soil will never hamper London Pride.

SCABIOSA - graceful plants with light-coloured flowers which mix effectively with plants of similar hues such as CAMPANULA, LAVENDER and GERANIUM and with those that will contrast for example HEUCHERA. Plant in a sunny spot in soil that is well-drained especially in winter. Recommended are:- S. CAUCASICA CLIVE GREAVES; long serrated grey-green leaves and stems 45cm (18") high with lavender-blue flowers. MISS WILLMOTT same height has creamy-white flowers. S. COLUMBARIA BUTTERFLY BLUE is around 30cm (12") high with grey-green leaves and lavender-blue flowers. The 'Pincushion flower' will perform from mid to late summer.

SEDUM - definitely worth including as they have a prescence in all the seasons. In early spring the plant's crown shows silvery-blue succulent shoots which develop into fleshy-leaved rosettes by late spring. During summer these elongate into leafy stems bearing clusters of tight flower buds and by late summer/early autumn resemble stalks of broccoli with tiny starry flowers. Even when the colour has faded the heads remain intact and during any winter hoar frost can again be an attractive feature. Flowers are a hit with hoverflies (whose larvae will enjoy any aphids that are around) and bees and butterflies; especially tortoiseshells. Grow in full sun in well-drained soil but do not enrich it too much because enthusiastic growth can lead to top-heavy floppy stems. Lift every 3-4 years and divide to ensure vibrant flowers. Recommended are:- S. HERBSTFREUDE (or AUTUMN JOY) opening from pale green buds into pink flowers which then darken to rose-pink and finally to reddish-brown. Glaucous mid-green stems and fleshy dark green leaves. Up to 60cm (24") high. Will combine effectively with DAHLIA BISHOP OF LLANDAFF, COTINUS COGGYGRIA ROYAL PURPLE, hip-bearing ROSES such as MOYESII GERANIUM and plants with silver leaves. S. RUBY GLOW grows to 25cm (10") high bearing ruby-red flowers with red stems and purple-green leaves, especially attractive in the vicinity of brick. S. TELEPHIUM MAXIMUM ATROPURPUREUM has glaucous red-brown stems and leaves with sprays of deep pink flowers reaching 45-60cm (18-24") high. A good associate for ALLIUM CRISTOPHII, GERANIUMS such as G. OXONIANUM WARGRAVE PINK or CLARIDGE DRUCE and COSMOS ATROSANGUINEUS. S. VERA JAMESON has purple stems and serrated glaucous plum-purple leaves. Flowers are of soft rose-pink and the plant is 20-30cm (8-12") in height. Blends well with LAVENDER and GERANIUM JOHNSON'S BLUE. S. SPECTABILE has green stems with serrated grey-green leaves and pale pink flowers (lovely with bluey-mauve CAMPANULAS and AGAPANTHUS). Variety BRILLIANT bears flowers which are made up of pink petals and slightly darker pink anthers. CARMEN is more mauve-pink. Both combine effectively with HEUCHERAS CHOCOLATE RUFFLES, PLUM PUDDIN and PALACE PURPLE accentuating their deep red foliage. ICEBERG has pea-green stems and leaves with pure white flowers. All 30-45cm (12-18") in height. JAPANESE ANEMONE, ASTRANTIA RUBY WEDDING and marmalade HELENIUM are further examples of plants which will be enhanced and contrasted through planting with sedum. Sedum stems are inclined to turn a buttery yellow in late autumn which gives a pleasant glow in the sunshine. S. ERYTHROSTICTUM FROSTY MORN has oval pale grey-green leaves edged with cream and pale pinky-white flowers. Up to 45cm (18") high.

SIDALCEA - ELSIE HEUGH bears flowers of a delightful pale pink: delicately fringed around the edges the petals appear to have the fragility of moth wings but are long-lasting and held on upright stems. SUSSEX BEAUTY is a deeper pink with a satiny texture the flowers borne on upright branching stems. Up to 90cm (36") high. Early into midsummer they are attractive in the company of pale blue AGAPANTHUS for example. Grow in organically enriched moist but well-drained soil in full sun. A dry mulch in winter would be appreciated and the plants are best lifted and divided every 3 years or so.

SILENE DIOICA - most garden centres have a section for 'wild flowers' and it is a good idea to mix both cultivated and wild plants to give the garden a natural feel. RED CAMPION is a plant that is worth intermingling in the border. The colour of the delicate little flowers is actually more of a deep pink and therefore will fit in with many of the plants already described especially ROSES and ASTRANTIA. You will need only one plant because it will make a lot of seed which will generate plenty of new plants for your needs. Obviously removing spent stems will minimise this. Height will be up to 100cm (40") and flowering will start around May and if spent stems are cut off (having set seed or not) the plant will make later flowers. Eventually discard woody plants for fresh self-seeded plants. Any sunny situation will do. WHITE CAMPION (SILENE ALBA) can be tried too; this is strongly scented attracting night-flying moths while the scentless red campion is pollinated by bumble bees and hoverflies. Both have hairy dark green leaves.

SOLIDAGO - any well-drained soil in sun or partial shade will suit GOLDEN ROD; a useful plant for its feathery sprays of tiny golden yellow flowers during late summer into early autumn. Giving contrast to performers such as HELENIUM, HELIOPSIS, HELIANTHUS, ACHILLEA, CROCOSMIA, COREOPSIS and FOENICULUM VULGARE PURPUREUM. Always go for a named plant as others can be invasive. Try S. GOLDENMOSA at 75cm (30") high with mid-green leaves and erect stems.

THALICTRUM - although tall vibrant and statuesque this plant is self-supporting and allows effective underplanting. Grow in organically enriched moisture retentive soil in partial shade. The glaucous shoots appear in mid to late spring followed by fine stems with ferny bluish mid-green foliage. Flowers during mid to late summer. Recommended are:- T. DELAVAYI reaching 1.2m (4') high with soft mauve stems and fluffy long-stalked mauve flowers with cream anthers. Variety ALBUM has an abundance of long-stalked fluffy white flowers on green stems while HEWITT'S DOUBLE has an explosion of bobble-like lilac flowers on grey stems. Effective with FOENICULUM VULGARE PURPUREUM and underplanted with HEUCHERA. Also with ECHINACEA, the slender stems of ALLIUMS and AGAPANTHUS, white PHLOX, the spires of LYTHRUM plus PIMPINELLA, COTINUS, ABIES KOREANA and ROSES.

TROLLIUS - the spring into summer flowering GLOBEFLOWERS are plants for a very moist patch in the garden either in sun or partial shade. Organic enrichment will be appreciated. Remove faded flower stems and feed with Blood, Fish and Bone in the hope of more flowers. These are borne on erect stems above mounds of deep green glossy leaves, the plant's common name tells you the flower's shape! Recommendations are all T. x CULTORUM cultivars:- ALABASTER with pale primrose-yellow flowers mid to late spring 60cm (24") high. EARLIEST OF ALL has clear buttercup-yellow flowers 50cm (20") high in mid-spring. LEMON QUEEN bears pale yellow flowers late spring into early summer while ORANGE PRINCESS has orangey-yellow blooms at the same time. Both 60cm (24") high.

VERBASCUM - these bring thrusting elegant spires to the mixed border and providing spent flower spikes are removed followed by an occasional dressing of Blood, Fish and Bone they will continue to flower throughout the summer. New plants can be created from ROOT CUTTINGS. Very well-drained soil in full sun or partial shade is required and a mulch of spent mushroom compost will be appreciated. Keep the centre of the plants free from dead leaves to deter rotting and make sure all flowering spikes are removed by mid-autumn so that the plant's energies go into building an overwintering crown without threat of disease entering from a decomposing spike. The plants may need staking in exposed areas. Recommended are:- V. CHAIXII ALBUM with grey-green hairy leaves at the base and pure white flowers with mauve centres densely arranged on branching 90cm (3') slender spikes. V. COTSWOLD QUEEN has erect spikes bearing deep yellow flowers with maroon centres 1.2m (4') above grey-green foliage. V GAINSBOROUGH is the same height and leaf colour with creamy-yellow flowers. Both would look good in the company of TROLLIUS. V. HELEN JOHNSON has sturdy spires of unusual caramel-coloured flowers with mauve stamens. The leaves are a furry grey-green and height is 90cm (3'). V. CHAIXII PINK DOMINO has blush-pink flowers with a darker pink centre on unbranched spikes 1.2m (4') high with dark purplish-green leaves. V. JACKIE has branched spikes of dusky-pink flowers 40cm (16") above grey-green foliage. Verbascums mix well with ROSES and PHLOX and are attractive to bees and hoverflies.

VERBENA BONARIENSIS - up to 2m (6') high strong upright slender branching stems with a few thin dark green leaves. At the top there are abundant clusters of tiny vibrant purple flowers which are enchanting in a breeze. This is a see-through plant giving height to the border but allowing the other plants to be in the picture. Its colour will easily compliment and contrast with theirs and melds well with bonfire or pastel shades. A BUDDLEJA such as LOCHINCH or ALTERNIFOLIA nearby would be complimentary in colour while giving a contrast of shape. Performs from midsummer to mid-autumn. Plant in moisture retentive well-drained soil in full sun. A dry organic mulch in winter could be beneficial but this is a plant which produces a lot of seed so once established it is likely you will have plenty of self-sets. These tend to appear randomly bringing a natural and ethereal air to the garden. Very popular with bees.

VIOLA ODORATA - the ENGLISH or SWEET VIOLET is worth planting at the base of a hedge or somewhere which is neither in deep shade nor hot sun; ideally in sun for about half a day. Dig some horticultural grit into the soil to improve drainage and give the soil plenty of organic enrichment by mulching to keep moisture in. Dressings of Blood, Fish and Bone would be beneficial. The evergreen leaves are bright green rounded to heart-shaped. In late winter/early spring depending on the variety either violet or white exquisitely sweetly scented flowers appear. When established will self-seed freely. Up to 20cm (8") high the plants are capable of spreading by underground stems known as RHIZOMES.

CHAPTER THIRTEEN
'FINE TUNING THE MIXED BORDER WITH GRASSES'

The perennials which you have planted will bring a wide variety of flower colour, shape and height to your border. All you need to do now is to get everything FLOWING in a GRACEFUL way. The power for this is the constantly changing light and motion of the air. The medium is GRASSES. A good example of how this works is a field of Barley. However beautiful the immediate scenery your attention is always drawn to the way the barley ripples in response to the breeze with a delightful swish, how scudding clouds restlessly fold and unfold shadows across the field, the manner in which the colour of the barley is illuminated in shafts of sunlight, stands out against a leaden sky, is enhanced through sunlight diffused by early morning mist or in the warm fading light of evening, how the light plays on raindrops or dew amplifies the hairy wispy textures. Grasses have unique flower forms and foliage while their texture, form, colour and outline gives them a distinctive prescence in the border while being season-long supporting acts for all the other players.

Grasses do not have flowers which are brightly coloured or scented simply because their pollen is transferred by the wind rather than insects. Of course they have flowers for pollen to be present but they are incredibly tiny and in vast numbers. They are held in a cluster called an INFLORESCENCE. This may be attached directly to the top of an unbranched narrow stem (a SPIKE) or by short stems extending from the top of the stem itself (a RACEME). The inflorescence may also have side branches (a PANICLE). The whiskery extensions to the inflorescence (like on barley) are called AWNS.

TIM'S CHOICE:-

STIPA TENNUISSIMA - it has been proved that stroking a cat is therapeutic especially for those suffering from stress (so if you spot the cat that has dug a hole in your border don't lob something at it - call it over, give it a stroke and you'll very calmly fork over the damage!). S. TENNUISSIMA (commonly known as the 'PONY TAIL' grass) has a very fine silky appearance - people cannot resist stroking it whenever they pass. So help for your wellbeing without having to buy cat food! More importantly this grass at 60cm (24") high is very effective throughout the border especially at the front where it can be touched and around ROSES to hide their not so attractive stems. It will wave delightfully in the slightest breeze and the panicles mature from greenish white to warm blonde. The plant will give pleasure right through to the winter until March when it can be cut to the ground allowing rapid new growth to begin. (During the winter the crown will have been protected by the stems). Plant in well-drained soil in full sun so it can be accentuated by the changing light.This is a plant that some sources overprice so be careful as it will self-seed and the little pony tails can be left for a natural effect or replanted somewhere else. For good effect underplant BIRCH with this grass as both respond to breeze and light.

STIPA GIGANTEA - this is a big plant which needs a space at least 90cm (36") in which to develop. Same conditions as S. tennuissima. Around 2m (6') in height. It makes a clump of evergreen grey-green leaves from which the erect, bristled, silvery, purplish-green spikes emerge about May. These will ripen to gold and bear airy golden oat-like flower panicles which shoot in all directions later in the summer and into autumn. Backlit by the sun this majestic plant casts a shimmering veil over the border. Wonderful in a hoar-frost too. Plants such as RUDBECKIA HERBSTSONNE, HELENIUMS, ECHINACEA PURPUREA and LAVENDER are good companions. ALLIUMS especially with their seedheads are especially effective. If you think your border could be overwhelmed by the 'GOLDEN OATS' grass you could consider it as a 'stand alone' plant perhaps in your grassed area. Remove spikes when they break down and in spring rake out any dead foliage from the clump just before the new growth begins.

STIPA ARUNDINACEA - known as the 'PHEASANT'S TAIL' grass this is evergreen with new growth drab olive-green maturing shiny pale green, then orange and red and finally orange-brown by late winter. From midsummer to early autumn arching pendent reddish panicles glow when backlit by the sun. Even in November this continues in the low light and in fact cold weather will intensify the colour. 60cm (24") high. Same planting conditions and care as S. gigantea. Will tolerate light shade. COREOPSIS, SEDUM, ACHILLEA and ECHINACEA will combine well.

MISCANTHUS SINENSIS - these grasses hold their form throughout the winter and in times of hoar-frost will appear quite magical. They also look attractive when backlit by low winter sunshine (which has the same photogenic effect as summer sunshine at dawn and dusk). When the new shoots reach 5-10cm (2-4") cut down the old stems carefully to avoid damage and remove any dead foliage. Well-drained soil in full sun or partial shade. ALL grasses will take a year or two to establish and will benefit from a little mulch to keep moisture in the soil. Grasses do not need additional feed which would cause them to become lush and limp. When the plants become congested (usually after 5-6 years) lift with your spade and use it or a BOW SAW* to slice through the root system. Discard the woody segments and replant new vigorous growth. This should be done late spring into very early summer. Miscanthus are particularly reflective of light and are good illuminators. This can be emphasised by planting against a darker background such as evergreens, purple leaved shrubs like COTINUS, also copper and purple BEECH.

ANNEX: 'TOOL UP!' - a BOW SAW is worth buying for this job but mainly for pruning work on your trees when they have matured. The blade is supported under tension between the two arms of a light metal 'bow' and cuts on both the push and pull of the sawing action which gets the job done quickly and with the minimum of effort. Replacement blades are available and it is always wise to buy the best you can afford from garden centres or ironmongers.

M.SINENSIS KLEINE SILBERSPINNE (translated as 'Little Silver Spider'). Reaches 90cm (3') high with open spidery silver-pink panicles from midsummer and narrow graceful foliage. Late summer into autumn the panicles mature to silver. Associates well with the flowers and foliage of SEDUM, LAVATERA, ALLIUM (especially the seedheads), ACONITUM, SOLIDAGO and BUDDLEJA.

M. SINENSIS MORNING LIGHT has white-edged green arching foliage which gives it a silvery effect by reflecting light. Branched flower clusters mature from reddish-brown to pinky-white. 1.2m (4') high. In autumn this grass turns golden and by winter it is the colour of straw. Excellent with pastel coloured ROSES.

M. TRANSMORRISONENSIS is an evergreen grass with narrow green arching foliage and 1.2m (4') branched spikes bearing reddish-brown flower clusters which become buff with age.

MOLINIA CAERULA ARUNDINACEA TRANSPARENT - for moisture retentive well-drained soil in sun or partial shade. A tall plant at 2m (6') high. Dark green leaves with erect but delicate flower spikes which are very attractive following rain or frost. And also in the vicinity of ERYNGIUM, ECHINACEA and ALLIUM CRISTOPHII with its metallic purple heads which mingle well with the molinia's purple flowers; these mature to golden yellow in autumn.

M. CAERULA ARUNDINACEA KARL FOERSTER is the same height with arching foliage and stems fanning out bearing purple flower spikes which also turn golden yellow in autumn. A plant which has a softening influence on the border and can also be used as a 'stand alone'. COTINUS COGGYGRIA ROYAL PURPLE is an attractive backdrop.

M. CAERULA VARIEGATA is 45-60cm (15-24") high and therefore suitable for the front of the border. Not surprisingly variegated cream and light green foliage - this turns yellow then tan in the autumn. The stems are yellow and the flower spikes bear purple tinted green panicles in midsummer maturing golden by the autumn. Plants such as COREOPSIS will make good symbiotic partners.

PANICUM VIRGATUM - HEAVY METAL is 1.2m (4') high with erect blue-grey leaves which turn bright yellow in the autumn and tawny in winter. During mid to late summer purple-pink flowers are borne in whispy finely branching panicles and these survive into winter. Well-drained soil in full sun.

P. VIRGATUM RUBRUM is 1m (3') high and the upper parts of the leaves are reddish-brown which intensifies during autumn. The flowers are a delicate greeny-brown. Looks very attractive arching over compact SEDUMS which have similar colour but contrasting shape.

PENNISETUM ALOPECUROIDES HAMELN - fountain-shaped grass 75cm (30") high for well-drained soil in full sun. Arching narrow rich green glossy leaves which mature to golden yellow in autumn and straw colour by winter. In July bears fluffy clusters of greenish-cream to pinkish bottlebrush-like flowers which become tan by autumn. These look very attractive when covered in dew and combine well with SCABIOSA,

GYPSOPHILA and VERBENA BONARIENSIS which is a wonderful partner for all grasses. As is THALICTRUM. Cut back in spring.

MILIUM EFFUSUM AUREA - for moist well-drained soil in partial shade ideally but will grow successfully in sun as long as the soil does not dry out. Evergreen 'BOWLES GOLDEN GRASS' as it is commonly known has bright lime-yellow foliage which combines well with HELLEBORES, HEUCHERAS and HOSTAS. A good reflector this grass will lighten up any area of dappled shade. Reaches 45cm (18") high with spikelets of suffused yellow delicate enough to catch the breeze. These airy seedheads are an effective contrast with those of ALLIUM while the preceding purple flowers look attractive against the milium's foliage.

CALAMAGROSTIS ACUTIFLORA KARL FOERSTER - is a tall growing grass at 1.8m (6') high and requires moisture retentive soil in sun or partial shade. Has lustrous green foliage and produces loose feathery light pink inflorescences during summer which tighten up as they change to a wheat colour. Remaining throughout winter this grass should be cut down when the new shoots are 10cm (4") high. A dramatic 'stand alone' plant and especially effective with LAVENDER, LAVATERA, GERANIUM, RUDBECKIA, SEDUM and CISTUS. Full sun will enable the grass to catch the light with striking results as the filimentous flowerheads bend in the breeze.

CAREX COMANS BRONZE - growing to 30cm (12") high the ever present swirl of hair-like bronze foliage is extremely effective in the company of yellow and orange flowers eg CROCOSMIA EMILY McKENZIE. Also with the leaves of ASTILBE and HEUCHERA and any pale green or silvery foliage where it gives obvious relief and glows in the sunshine. Grow in well-drained soil in full sun. In spring comb out by hand any loose dead foliage.

CHASMANTHIUM LATIFOLIUM - known as 'WOOD OATS' because of the flattened oat-like spikelets which dangle on the slender 1m (36") light green stems during summer. They start green and turn to red-bronze in autumn and finally to pinkish-buff through winter, Light green leaves turn to copper-brown in autumn. Grow in moisture retentive well-drained soil in sun or partial shade cutting down by late winter. The pendent seedheads are delightful in a breeze.

HELICTOTRICHON SEMPERVIRENS - this one is the 'BLUE OAT GRASS' a dense 'evergreen' clump of erect blue-grey foliage. Early to midsummer stiff stems 1.4m (4½') high hold shimmering greenish-tan purple-marked oat-like panicles which nod in the breeze. Plant in well-drained soil in full sun to intensify colour removing old stems and combing out dead leaves in spring. Blue grasses blend very effectively with pastel flowers and foliage for example FOXGLOVES, COREOPSIS, PHLOX, JAPANESE ANEMONE, HELIANTHUS, ERYNGIUM, ROSES (especially with blue grey-green foliage), PANICUM VIRGATUM, LYCHNIS, RUDBECKIA, ALLIUMS, SEDUM, AGAPANTHUS and LAVENDER.

FESTUCA GLAUCA ELIJAH BLUE - has all the blending qualities of Helictotrichon but with a height of just 30cm (12"). A spiky dome of fine silver-blue foliage and stems bearing blue-green panicles during early summer. Very attractive when backlit by sunshine and in a breeze. Same conditions and procedure as Helictotrichon except that every 2-3 years Elijah blue should be cut right back, lifted, divided and replanted to maintain the colour. Excellent with GERANIUMS such as RUSSELL PRITCHARD.

HAKONECHLOA MACRA AUREOLA - or the 'GOLDEN HAKONE GRASS'. A dense low mound of gracefully arching slender leaves which are bright yellow with narrow green stripes gaining a red tinge by autumn which lasts into winter. Partial shade will produce the most intense leaf colour and the soil should be moisture retentive but well-drained. When necessary divide and replant in late spring. From late summer to mid-autumn bears fine pale green spikelets in open panicles on stems 35 cm (14") high. If your garden has a steepish slope plant a series of these grasses the second below the first from the top down and so on as their shape will create a dramatic 'waterfall' effect. Will look very attractive with the same companions as MILIUM EFFUSUM AUREUM, also purple or yellow leafed trees and shrubs, ALCHEMILLA MOLLIS (excellent along the edge of a path to soften its impact), blue/purple flowers such as CAMPANULA and GERANIUM. A great illuminator in shady areas.

CHAPTER FOURTEEN
'ADDING BULBS FOR THE COMPLETE SPRING SCENE'

Come September garden centres, shops and mail order specialists will be offering spring bulbs for sale. The sight of snowdrops in bloom always sends a jolt of excitement through the winter weary while the first daffodils will be confirmation for many that "spring's here!". In autumn dormant bulbs may not look very exciting but they are ingenious performers with huge sensual and aesthetic impact which makes them major participants in any garden.

A bulb is basically all the components of a flowering plant - roots, leaves, stem and flower bud in an undeveloped state within a casing of thick fleshy tissues loaded with water and concentrated starch. The scaly brown covering is protection against insects and soil micro-organisms. Bulbs multiply by producing bulblets which develop from buds that form around the base of the bulb. In time these will bulk-up and be capable of flowering themselves. Bulbs are priced according to size simply because the larger the bulb the greater its flower power. It is important to FEEL bulbs when buying as firmness equals fitness. During the first weeks after planting bulbs will take in moisture to replenish what has been lost while they have been out of the ground. Roots will begin to strike out in search of nutrients to sustain leaf growth. The concentrated starch initially acts as an antifreeze protecting the bulb from damage but as temperatures rise it begins to convert into energy-rich sugars to feed the developing plant. Bulbs will appreciate a dose of Blood, Fish and Bone when growth appears above ground for immediate nourishment and for next years embryonic flower buds in the heart of the bulb. Some of the roots respond to gravity and pull the bulb into the best position possible even ensuring it is the right way up!

TIM'S TIPS FOR BUYING BULBS

DAFFODILS - look out for double or triple 'nosers' - these are like two or three bulbs joined together (actually one bulb with flowering size bulblets attached). Each bulb has a 'nose' from which a flowering stem will emerge. So more flower power for your money. Do try and get your daffodils planted as soon as you can. Even if a few days are going to elapse storage is critical. Those bought in ventilated plastic bags attached to a descriptive/pictorial card are OK but loose bulbs in plastic carriers etc will very quickly sweat and go soft. Transfer these to a net bag or into a pair of old tights. Ideally hang or place in a room with low humidity and a constant cool temperature. Paper bags/cardboard containers are just about all right for short periods in these conditions but if you are storing in a shed/garage the paper wlll rapidly absorb enough moisture to cause the bulbs to go soft.

SNOWDROPS/WINTER ACONITES/FRITILLARIA MELEAGRIS - the problem with these bulbs is that when out of the ground they can sometimes lose enough moisture to actually go past the point of no return. So to be on the safe side buy these 'IN THE GREEN' when you see advertisements for them in the gardening and weekend press around February. Make sure these are from cultivated stock and not nicked from the wild. These bulbs will have been lifted when their flowers have finished and you will receive them within days leaves and all. Plant as soon as you can at the same depth they were growing prior to lifting - notice the stem colour; the green section is above ground the white bit below.

HYACINTHS - there are three categories for sale; 'top size', 'bedding' and 'prepared'. 'Top size' are really for potting up for inside the house. For garden use 'bedding' is what you need. 'Prepared' are for potting up for an early show in the house (these have been subjected to a regime of controlled temperature which causes them to flower around Christmas).

TULIPS - the one species of bulb that so long as they are in good condition and well stored can be left until late October before planting.

SMALL BULBS e.g. CROCUS, MUSCARI, SCILLAS, ANEMONE BLANDA - buy as early as you can and get them planted as quickly as possible to minimise loss of moisture. Crocus though rarely come to any harm if stored correctly and start shooting early which gives a clue to which way up they should be planted!

TIM'S CHOICE:-

SNOWDROPS - have evolved to cope with the worst of winter weather with shoots sharp enough to pierce frozen ground. The design of their flowers allows snow and raindrops to slide off easily without harming the all important reproductive parts of the flower. Leave the flowers to set and shed seed which will form new bulbs in addition to those developing from the bulb itself. Snowdrops are best grouped in soil rich in organic matter which does not dry out during summer but is well-drained. Heavy soils would benefit from some added horticultural grit. Dappled shade is ideal but sunny borders will suffice. The lime in spent mushroom compost makes it a good choice for a mulch and a dressing of Blood, Fish and Bone will be welcomed in autumn. Snowdrops generally take a year or two to establish and attain full flower power. They do look very attractive when planted in drifts in grass. Lift a square of grass; dig the hole and fork over the bottom placing the bulbs in and replacing the soil with an incorporation of Blood, Fish and Bone. Then put the turf back. Snowdrops planted this way may take a little longer to establish. Remember you will not be able to cut the grass for six weeks after flowering to allow the seed to disperse and the leaves to photosynthesise and feed the bulbs. A dressing of Blood, Fish and Bone will be beneficial both to the snowdrops and the grass following flowering.

The botanical name for snowdrops is 'GALANTHUS' which comes from the Greek 'gala' = milk and 'anthos' = flower. There are hundreds of varieties but whichever ones you have do put a hand lens over the flower and be enchanted by the delicate green 'brush strokes'. They are all scented. Recommended are:- G. NIVALIS the common snowdrop which should be planted 5cm (2") deep and apart. G. MAGNET is vigorous, robust and reliable especially in grass. Plant 12cm (5") deep. Combines effectively if planted under HAMAMELIS such as PALLIDA and in the company of HELLEBORUS especially those with greenish hues, also CYCLAMEN COUM and HEDERIFOLIUM whose leaves will be especially complimentary. The foliage of PULMONARIA e.g. LEWIS PALMER is a good symbiotic partner. G. ELWESII is another robust variety with a honey scent and should be planted at the same depth as MAGNET. G. S. ARNOTT is also strongly scented with large flowers requiring the deeper planting and establishes quickly. Further snowdrop partners include white stemmed BIRCH and contrasting red-barked dogwood CORNUS ALBA SIBIRICA.

WINTER ACONITE:- ERANTHIS HYEMALIS requires the same conditions as snowdrops and planting at 12cm (2") deep. Produces bright yellow buttercup-like flowers above a frilly ruff of bright green leaves 5-8cm (2-3") high. A very poisonous plant indeed which has been put to dark use in the past! As one of the first brightly coloured spring flowers it is a useful source of nectar for any pollinating insects taking advantage of a sunny early spring day. Add winter aconites to the symbiotic partners suggested for snowdrops. KERRIA JAPONICA would look very attractive underplanted with these little flowers. Allow to seed and mulch with spent mushroom compost and you should get a good carpet of winter aconites in a fairly short time.

CROCUS:- these bulbs are ideal for planting in drifts in the grass or under trees and spring flowering shrubs. The many different colours that are available make symbiotic association easy. Their flowers are shaped like little hot air balloons and open on sunny days for pollination but close at sundown or during inclement weather to protect their reproductive parts. The air in these little balloons will be warmer than outside which helps to produce more nectar - a boon for early spring pollinators. Plant 8-10cm (3-4") deep and 5cm (2") apart in soil prepared as for snowdrops but in a sunny or lightly shaded spot. Allow leaves to photosynthesise for six weeks after flowering before removing. Recommended are:- DUTCH YELLOW producing orangey-yellow flowers a plenty, C. TOMMASINIANUS varieties BARR'S PURPLE (purple flowers tinged silver on the outsides), RUBY GIANT (reddish-purple flowers) and WHITEWELL PURPLE (reddish-purple flowers with silvery-mauve insides). YELLOW GIANT has a prolific display of bright yellow flowers, PICKWICK a purple base to the flowers which are white heavily veined with purple, REMEMBRANCE with shimmering violet flowers, JEANNE D'ARC purple based flowers which are white with a feint purple hue, QUEEN OF THE BLUES with silvery deep mauve flowers and prominent orange stigmas. Sometimes yellow crocus come under attack from pecking Sparrows and Blackbirds and newly emerged crocus shoots from mice! Height 8-12cm (3-5")

ANEMONE BLANDA WHITE SPLENDOUR - the WIND FLOWER growing to 12cm (5") high with a profusion of long-lasting glistening pure white daisy-like flowers with pink-tinged backs. Plant 5cm (2") deep and 7cm (3") apart in well-drained organically enriched soil in sun or partial shade where they should quickly form a good carpet. Under seasonal shrubs is ideal. Especially effective if you can plant in the vicinity of the red-barked DOGWOOD and ASTILBE whose emerging vibrant red foliage will provide a stunning contrast. Also underneath white stemmed

BIRCH. Allow to set seed and leave undisturbed.

FRITILLARIA MELEAGRIS the 'SNAKE'S HEAD FRITILLARY'; best for a damp area of grass or moisture retentive soil with plenty of organic enrichment in full sun or partial shade. Variety ALBA is pure white while there are plenty of hybrids giving flowers of speckled rose and purple. The flowers are like little lanterns and are up to 30cm (12") high; a breeze will cause them to nod delightfully. Allow to set seed and leave undisturbed. Plant 5cm (2") deep and 7cm (3") apart. Symbiotically great with the flowers of HELLEBORUS, underneath seasonal shrubs and near leaves of CYCLAMEN COUM/HEDERIFOLIUM.

LEUCOJUM - snowdrops on steroids! L. AESTIVUM GRAVETYE GIANT can reach up to 90cm (36") if the soil is very moist, cool and organically enriched. Plant 8-10cm (3-4") deep and 10cm (4") apart. A profusion of pure white bells with yellowish-green tips. Allow to set seed and leave undisturbed. Known also as 'SNOWFLAKES'.

SCILLA SIBERICA SPRING BEAUTY - has lots of little bright deep blue bowl-shaped pendent flowers on stems 20cm (8") high. Well-drained organically enriched soil in sun or partial shade. Plant 8-10cm (3-4") deep. Allow to set seed and leave undisturbed for attractive spreading drifts.

MUSCARI ARMENIACUM - known as the 'GRAPE HYACINTH' for its spikes of tubular flowers. Several bulbs will create a carpet of bright blue flowers 20cm (8") high within a few years making them ideal for drifts of colour. So leave to self-seed. Plant 10cm (4") deep in organically enriched moist but well-drained soil in full sun. Although spring flowering the leaves appear in late autumn. HEAVENLY BLUE is a lovely bright blue. Will look very attractive in the company of SCILLAS and PULMONARIA e.g. LEWIS PALMER.

HYACINTHUS ORIENTALIS - or HYACINTH. For intense fragrance these must be included within the spring border. Plant 10cm (4") deep at least 8cm (3") apart in well-drained organically enriched soil in sun or partial shade. Spikes can be up to 20cm (8") high and covered with a profusion of tubular bell-shaped flowers. To benefit the most from the scent plant in a sheltered spot near to paths, doors and windows.

Hyacinths are often bought as growing bulbs in pots as gifts. When they (or any bulbs for that matter) have been enjoyed plant them 'in the green' outside with a dose of Blood, Fish and Bone to nourish them. If the bulbs were Christmas flowerers i.e. 'prepared' then they will take up to eighteen months to recover from the treatment and get up to full flower power. Recommended are:- OSTARA - violet-blue flowers with an almost black stem, BLUE JACKET - deep blue flowers with a slight silver tinge, DELFT BLUE - soft blue flowers, CARNEGIE - pure white, L'INNOCENCE - snow-white, LADY DERBY - rose-pink flowers, PINK PEARL - rose-pink flowers which attain a silver sheen with ageing and CHINA PINK whose flowers are blossom-pink which matures to blush-pink. Remove faded spikes.

HYACINTHOIDES NON-SCRIPTA - otherwise known as the ENGLISH BLUEBELL and worth including in an area of dappled shade to enjoy one of the country's best loved flowers at close quarters. Plant 8cm (3") deep in organically enriched moist but well-drained soil. Bluebells can be invasive so when you have enough remove faded flowers before they set and shed seed. The name 'bluebell' says it all apart from that they are scented and can actually come white! The flowers are all on one side of the stem and the top bends over. Can be bought mail-order 'in the green'. Always check when buying bluebells that they are from cultivated stock and not nicked from the wild. Height 20-30cm (8-12")

DAFFODILS - or NARCISSUS to give them their botanical name. The essence of springtime proper. Will cope with most conditions but do best in organically enriched well-drained soil which retains enough moisture to keep the bulbs plump during dormancy. In sun or partial shade but in a sheltered position preferably as daffodils are prone to snap in winds which can blight springtime these days. Ideal for planting in grass or borders in drifts as explained for snowdrops but at a depth of 3½ x the height of the bulb two to three bulb widths apart. Moisture on the grass becomes an atmospheric vapour at nightfall (dew) which keeps both leaves and flowers fresh. Bulbs in general produce many leaves and flowers and during a dry spring will appreciate some water during the evening. Remember the grass cannot be cut for six weeks (unless the leaves have yellowed) following flowering to allow the leaves to photosynthesise. Spent flower heads (not stems) should be removed to stop the bulb trying to make a seed pod.

This energy is far better spent on building up strength within the bulb; producing bulblets and embryonic buds for next year. It is a common sight in late spring to see daffodil foliage trussed up by tidy-minded gardeners. This reduces the leaf area available for photosynthesis thereby depriving the bulb of some worthwhile food. From dormancy to a flowering plant in a few months takes some energy! An application of Blood, Fish and Bone would be advantageous at this time. Yellow daffodils blend easily within the spring garden but blue flowers e.g. PULMONARIA, SCILLA, MUSCARI, CROCUS and HYACINTH are particularly attractive partners. So are daffodils in the company of PRUNUS SERRULA with its glistening mahogany-like red/brown bark, against the shiny dark green branches of ABIES KOREANA, underneath the twisted branches of CORYLUS AVELLANA CONTORTA or below the pure white flowers of CHAENOMELES 'NIVALIS'. GRASSES too are a wonderful foil for daffodils. Lift, divide and replant daffodils (or any bulbs) when they lose vigour or become congested. There are many, many varieties of daffodils but here are some favourites chosen for weather resistance and maximum impact:-

TETE-A-TETE - growing up to 20cm (8") high makes this variety less likely to be wind damaged. Between 1-3 miniature trumpet daffodils on each strong stem gives a lot of colour for a few bulbs. Good for drifts in grass. Increases quickly. Buttercup-gold trumpets and pure yellow petals.

FEBRUARY GOLD - does well in grass and bulks up quickly. 30cm (12") high. Deep golden yellow longish trumpet with a frilly edge and pure yellow swept-back petals.

JACK SNIPE - 20cm (8") high with slightly swept-back white petals and short lemon-yellow trumpets. Sturdy and increases rapidly.

JENNY - graceful swept-back satiny pure white petals and pale primrose trumpets that mature to cream. Ideal around white stemmed BIRCH, white and pastel coloured HELLEBORUS, DAPHNE ALBA, LONICERA STANDISHII, OSMANTHUS DELAVAYI etc. 30cm (12") high.

JETFIRE - swept-back golden yellow petals and long bright orange trumpets. 25cm (10") high.

SWEETNESS - 40cm (16") high with strongly scented velvety golden yellow flowers making it one for a sheltered spot for its own safety and for trapping the fragrance.

QUAIL - another one for an enclosed area as it too is fragrant and the same height as Sweetness. 2-3 golden yellow flowers with long trumpets per stem. A strong grower.

LIBERTY BELLS - 2-3 nodding deep lemon-yellow flowers per sturdy stem . 30cm (12") high.

TREVITHIAN - fine perfume and 45cm (18") high so you know where to plant! 1-3 soft lemon-yellow flowers per stem.

ST KEVERNE - rich golden yellow flowers with small trumpets. 45cm (18") high. Very reliable.

TULIPS - bring wonderful colours in the most stately of ways to the border mid to late spring. Well-drained soil in full sun is essential and if the ground gets a good baking in the summer then this will pay dividends. Tulips differ from the other bulbs in that the following years leaves and flowers come from new bulblets. An application of Blood, Fish and Bone at planting time will be beneficial. As well as slugs and snails which can eat emerging shoots on all bulbs thereby damaging the flowers, tulips are prone to a fungal disease called tulip fire. As the foliage dies down it can become infected with fungal spores of the disease so called because the following year's flowers give the appearance of being scorched by fire. To minimise the risk plant the bulbs 20cm (8") deep. Spores are unlikely to reach bulbs at this depth. Tulip bulbs can always be the very last to go in and if there has been a hard frost or two this should have killed any fungal spores which could have been lurking in the top 5cm (2") of soil. When the flowers are spent remove them from the tops of the stems and gather any fallen petals to stop any spores going into the soil. Similarly as soon as the foliage goes yellow get rid of it. Tulips are particularly effective planted in groups so dig out a large hole to the right depth and put 2.5cm (1") of horticultural grit into the base for added drainage. Then back-fill with the soil and some more grit scattered in as you go. Any fungul disease is more likely to take hold in humid conditions which are created by poor air circulation. So that air can circulate around the plants plant the bulbs about 10cm (4") apart.

Tulip flowers appear to shimmer in spring sunshine. Red tulips are especially attractive in the company of dark leaved HEUCHERAS such as PALACE PURPLE, LAMIUM BEACON SILVER, HOSTA ANTIOCH, LYSIMACHIA FIRECRACKER and the red barked dogwood CORNUS ALBA SIBIRICA. Grasses such as MILIUM EFFUSUM AUREA and CAREX COMANS BRONZE will blend well too. All tulip flowers open wide on sunny days to attract pollinators but during inclement weather are closed to protect their reproductive parts. Although it is wise to plant tulips in as sheltered a spot as possible they unlike daffodils tend to sway rather than snap and raindrops simply run off the closed flowers. Because there is such an immense range of tulip colours, shapes and heights I am not going to recommend specific names but leave it to your personal choice and symbiotical imagination.

I will however recommend two plants that are worth including not just with tulips but within the spring garden as a whole. MYOSOTIS the 'FORGET-ME-NOT' and ERYSIMUM better known as the 'WALLFLOWER'. Both can be obtained from garden centres or local ironmongers/greengrocers during the autumn.

MYOSOTIS ALPESTRIS grows to 20cm (8") high and so you know how many to buy 15cm (6") across. The leaves are bright green and lance/spoon-shaped. Very dainty flowers are held in dense clusters and are bright blue with tiny yellow centres and bloom from spring into early summer. This is a one-off purchase for it self-seeds and in future years you can simply weed out or replant the self-sets. Discard when it has shed seed. A lovely associate for all colours of bulbs and spring flowering shrubs. M. SYLVATICA has lance-shaped hairy grey-green leaves and saucer-shaped tiny blue flowers with yellow centres. Grow in moist well-drained soil in full sun ideally with some shade from midday or in partial shade. There are several varieties with different intensities of blue. Ideal for border edgings.

WALLFLOWERS can be bought in mixed or specific colours. Fragrance is legendary and although pastel colours are now available shades of yellow, red and orange are the most familiar easily complimenting or contrasting with bulbs. 25-60cm (10-24") high. Space 30cm (12") apart. Grow in well-drained soil in full sun and discard when they have finished flowering. Flowers are held on short spikes and bloom from March to May. A mulch of spent mushroom compost will be appreciated for its lime content. Plant where the scent can be contained and appreciated. The prescence of wallflower and forget-me-not plants in the winter garden are always a heartening reminder of the coming joys of spring.

CHAPTER FIFTEEN
'ADDING ANNUALS FOR THE COMPLETE SUMMER PICTURE'

Fact is the impact annuals make on a garden in terms of colour, scent, shape, form and texture means you could probably win a 'best kept garden' competition with annuals alone. Honestly some people do. See their gardens when the annuals have gone and it is a very blank canvas indeed. Not the 365 day garden of interest which we are creating. Assigning annuals roles within a garden of many players actually intensifies the impact of all of them. As well as the garden as a whole.

The colour of a perennial's flowers for example can be emphasised if it is adjacent to an annual whose leaves/flowers are either a lighter or darker shade. The effect of linking annuals and perennials by colour is maintained for longer if the perennials can produce a succession of flowers. A well looked after annual can flower for a long time so with imagination could potentially interact with several perennials blooming at different times through the season. Linking annuals and perennials with foliage achieves season-long effect because leaves are simply around longer than flowers. Annuals with small to medium flowers can be used to relieve the dominance of some perennials while highlighting them at the same time. Annuals bring in a profusion of bees and butterflies, along with hoverflies and lacewings whose larvae feed on aphids. Annuals amongst ROSES not only hide the rather unattractive rose stems but could also introduce some diners to keep the roses aphid free!

The only way that you can have the majority of annuals is to grow them from seed. Pay a visit to the garden centre, ironmongers or large supermarket. Here you will find racks of packeted seeds in alphabetical order. Also trays (large ones are best) and pots (9-10cm (3½-4") will do) for sowing them into. You will of course need some 'seed sowing compost'. There is quite a choice! I would recommend any brand of compost made according to the formula and standards of the John Innes Horticultural Research Institute. The bag will have the John Innes Manufacturers Association Seal of Approval on it stating that it is for sowing seeds and rooting cuttings. This is the nearest to your garden soil but free of any disease or microorganisms which could attack and kill vulnerable new plants. It is made up of loam (basically clay and organic matter), peat (retains moisture, helps with drainage and air circulation while making humus as it decomposes), grit (for drainage and plant anchorage) and fertiliser (nitrogen for leaves, phosphates for roots, potash for flower development and trace elements for colour). For the record there are 3 further John Innes POTTING composts 1, 2 and 3: the higher the number the higher the fertiliser content. So as plants mature they need a higher number.

Then there are 'soil-less' composts which are either based on peat or alternatives such as coir (coconut fibre) and processed tree bark. All liberally laced with plant nutrients to correct their natural inertness. Basically peat is a unique form of organic matter consisting mainly of plant remains which have only partially decomposed because of lack of oxygen in conditions of high moisture. A special ecosystem of flora and fauna has evolved within these peat bogs and concern over its destruction when peat is removed inspired the creation of the alternatives. I wish they were as good or better but sadly not so! Mainly they fail to retain moisture as efficiently as peat; if too much is lost it is difficult to rehydrate causing big problems for little plants whose soft fleshy leaves transpire water very quickly. Also the added nutrients do not appear to work as well in these composts or last as long. And while peat makes humus as it decomposes the base materials of these composts tend to break down through the chemical action of bacteria leading to disease which is the last thing your seedlings need. Decomposing bark actually takes nitrogen OUT of the medium. Coir obviously covers many environmentally unfriendly air miles to get to this country from its source. Sometimes on the salty side but good at retaining water if not nutrients. However like it or not it seems that soil-less composts of the future will contain a gradually diminishing amount of peat. VERMICULITE is the end-product of heating a type of clay to 1000 degrees centigrade for a minute which causes the mineral to expand into a sterile open lattice structure with a dry spongy feel. Added to composts it will help to retain both water and nutrients and improve drainage. Available at garden centres.

TIM'S CHOICE OF BORDER ANNUALS:-

There is a lot of really useful information on seed packets. An accurate picture and description of what you will get along with instructions and tips for successful sowing, growing and planting. Choosing individual varicties is fun and a good grounding in symbiotic planting. So this list is to help you home in on plants which are easy to raise giving you satisfaction and pleasure, and your summer garden completeness and stimulation. Before filling your basket remember lots of packets mean lots of trays and pots; have you enough warm well-lit windowsills or space for wallpapering tables behind those windowsills or enough greenhouse benching? Sowing seeds is easy and fairly quick. It is when they become plants that they need your time. Time which is on top of what your garden itself asks of you. How much available space is there in the garden? (say where the spring bulbs have knocked off for the year). Honest answers will save you from chasing your tail or ending up with a drawer full of unopened seed packets with 'sow by' dates soon to be in the history books!

CALENDULA - daisy-style flowers mainly in oranges and lemons. Grow in a light airy spot to lessen chances of powdery mildew. Watch out for aphids (which can actually be eaten by wasps proving that they do in fact do something useful apart from winding people up!). Good with purple leaved SEDUM. ART SHADES 60cm (24") high includes apricot, orange and cream hues.

CALIFORNIAN POPPY - look for ESCHSCHOLZIA. Nice ferny light to blue-green foliage and delicate cupped flowers in pinks and citrus colours. Happy in poor soil. Ideally sow where they will flower as they do not favour transplanting. Varieties from 20-30cm (8-12") tall.

CLARKIA - delicate satiny pastel-coloured hollyhock-like flowers. Does not transplant easily. Varieties from 30-90cm (1-3') high.

CORNFLOWER - a special shade is 'cornflower blue' and there are lots of powder-puff like flowers on wiry stems with thin grey-green leaves. A light airy spot to try and avoid powdery mildew. Attractive to butterflies and bees. BLUE DIADEM and BLUE BALL 75cm (30") high are lovely.

COSMOS - daisy-like/saucer-shaped flowers borne on slender stems with delicate ferny foliage in shades of pink, white and red all with yellow centres. Excellent for blending with ROSES and ALLIUMS. Take precautions against slugs/snails especially with young plants. SENSATION MIXED bearing large single heads and SEASHELLS MIXED with petals shaped like fluted yellow-centred shells are worth getting. 120cm (48") high. Strong stemmed SONATA SERIES at 60cm (24") makes it ideal for windy spots.

FOXGLOVE - look under DIGITALIS. These were covered under perennials but it is worth getting some seeds while you are looking at the rack. They are unlikely to flower the year they are sown but will do so the following summer. Try apricot foxgloves near GRASSES for effect. Sow on the surface of a mixture of 50% John Innes No.2 and 50% seed sowing compost which is a good base for all biennials/perennials.

GODETIA - erect leafy spikes are topped by clusters of funnel-shaped flowers with a tissue paper texture. Shades of pink, white, apricot and red. Varieties from 30-45cm (12-18").

GYPSOPHILA - worth buying a packet of one of the annual varieties as its dainty, starry white flowers levitating above clouds of grey-green foliage contrasts with flowers of more dramatic colour and size. Some spent mushroom compost in the soil will provide some welcome lime. Try G. ELEGANS MONARCH WHITE 45cm (18").

HOLLYHOCK - an easy and cheap way of getting these lovely plants which are so attractive to bees. Covered under perennials.

HORDEUM JUBATUM - this is the 'SQUIRREL TAIL GRASS' and an annual. During summer it produces beautiful arching long-bristled, silky, barley-like tails that nod and glisten in the sun. They start off pale green flushed purple and mature to the colour of pale straw. Should self-seed for next year. 50cm (20") high for well-drained soil in full sun. Attractive in the company of DAHLIA DAVID HOWARD. Also intermingled with veils of GYPSOPHILA where the grass will highlight the softness of the white.

IPOMOEA - better known as 'MORNING GLORY' and there is no better variety than I. TRICOLOUR HEAVENLY BLUE. The colour is almost unmatched in plants - really sky-blue. Flowers are large (up to 10cm (4") across) and trumpet-shaped with white central tubes golden at the base. This is a climbing/scrambling plant and it will make rapid progress in a sheltered spot in full sun. The leaves are heart-shaped and light to mid-green. The flowers not surprisingly will greet you in the morning but will have faded by late afternoon; however it makes a vast number of them from July to October. An annual that needs to be sown later than all the others (end of May) because exposure to any chill can really damage this plant's chances of success. Quick growth will see them ready for the great outdoors and ideal summer temperatures. Take precautions against slugs and snails and remove spent flowers regularly. Keep well watered. Before sowing soak the seeds overnight before giving each one a 8cm (3") pot to grow in. When planting give the plant a directional idea by twining it round a cane pointed towards its destination!

LARKSPUR - a cottage garden favourite with its erect spikes densely covered with flowers usually in pastel tones. Reminiscent in appearance to Hyacinths echoed in two varieties - HYACINTH DWARF (50cm (20") high) and GIANT HYACINTH (60-90cm (24-36") high. In exposed gardens the lower growing varieties could be a good bet, otherwise stake. Take precautions against slugs, snails and powdery mildew.

LAVATERA - the annual mallow is a nice little bushy plant covered in large long-lasting trumpet-shaped flowers in hues of pink and white. MONT BLANC (60cm (24") high) glistens with snow-white flowers while SILVER CUP the same height has radiant pink trumpets with silvery veins.

NASTURTIUM - extremely easy to grow even in poor soil and a huge range of mainly bonfire colours. Ideal for scrambling and climbing through the border. Funnel-shaped flowers with five distinct petals and rounded leaves on long stalks which anchor the plant as it makes its way around to a distance of up to 180cm (72"). The only drawbacks are the caterpillars of cabbage-white butterflies which can decimate the foliage along with black fly. Removing the infected leaves at an early stage will help to keep the plants thriving. Nasturtiums can make an attractive feature scrambling up the sunny side of a hedge. There are non-scramblers which are around 30cm (12") high.

NICOTIANA - the 'TOBACCO PLANT' noted for its intense fragrance especially in the evening. Ideal for the back of borders is N. SYLVESTRIS which reaches up to 1.5m (5') with several strong branches bearing graceful clusters of scented, nodding, elongated tubular pure white flowers. If you can have perennials nearby whose foliage is marked with silver or white they will be symbiotically enhanced e.g. HOSTA MOONLIGHT. Appropriately such variegated foliage reflects actual moonlight and is intensified. Pale ROSES and white FOXGLOVES will contribute even more. Moonlight also accentuates the shape of flowers. Blue flowers will emphasise the coolness of white. N. Sylvestris needs rich, moist soil. White is given further prominence in the vicinity of green. N. LIME GREEN (75cm (30") high) has trumpet-shaped flowers and a lovely perfume; a great partner for N. SYLVESTRIS and for DAHLIAS such as MURDOCH and CLAIR DE LUNE. GRASSES e.g. HAKONECHLOA MACRA AUREOLA will also make effective companions. Watch out for aphids.

NIGELLA - known as 'LOVE-IN-A-MIST' the misty blue flowers have filigree whiskery green ruffs and nestle amongst bright green ferny foliage. Blue is a restful colour and from a distance these plants give the illusion of a soft blue mist. MISS JEKYLL is a lovely pale blue which goes well with CORNFLOWERS and GRASSES e.g. STIPA TENUISSIMA. 45cm (18") high. The seed pods which hold generous amounts of seed for self-sets are extremely pretty in their own right. A packet of one of the deeper blues would be a nice accompaniment. These have bluey-purple seed pods. Wonderful partners for ROSES and most effective in drifts.

NIGHT SCENTED STOCK - probably under MATTHIOLA BICORNIS. Only 30cm (1') high and not the most exciting of pale lilac flowers by day but a wonderful clove-like scent is released at night when the flowers fully open. The warmer the weather the more intense the scent. Best grown in clumps where you can appreciate the fragrance at close quarters.

POPPY - look under PAPAVER and you will find a wonderful array of these brightly coloured, ethereal stalwarts of English cottage gardens. The stems are wiry and when hairy are accentuated by dew or raindrops. Buds are pendent and flowers either bowl, cup or saucer-shaped which open as wide as possible. Seed pods are a notable feature looking like little pepper pots which sow their copious quantities of seed as the stem sways in the breeze. Bees will bob from flower to flower within a medley of poppies and some attractive cross-pollinated seedlings may come up as a result. Unexpected discoveries are not just exciting but often found growing in symbiotic ways that had not occurred to the gardener! To keep the plants blooming remove some of the spent flowers before they set seed. Poppy seeds are able to lie dormant for years only germinating when there has been soil disturbance. The following are certainly worth coming home with:- P. COMMUTATUM LADYBIRD - brilliant red flowers with large black spots, 45cm (18") in height and an effective partner with CROCOSMIA LUCIFER, DAHLIA BISHOP OF LLANDAFF and GRASSES. P. RHOEAS 'SHIRLEY' series has petals like tissue paper, others like crumpled tissue paper! Colours include yellow, pink, orange and red. The wild red cornfield poppy (P. RHOEAS itself) has a place too especially in drifts. P. RHOEAS FAIRY WINGS produces flowers in shades of grey-pink, soft pink and pale mauve. Attractive with ASTRANTIA and VERBASCUM. All 60cm (24") high. P. SOMNIFERUM is actually the opium poppy but its garden varieties (and the British climate) will not yield anything more exciting than beautiful flowers! PAEONY FLOWERED has large, frilly tissue-papery flowers in colours including red, lilac, pink, salmon-pink, white and maroon-red. The tallest annual poppies at 90cm (36"). Do not try and transplant poppies.

STOCKS - likely to come under MATTHIOLA and a must for glorious scent combined with spikes of densely clustered flowers in hues of pink, purple and white. M. INCANA CINDERELLA series grows between 20-25cm (8-10") tall with a branching habit giving several flower spikes. M. INCANA TEN WEEK MIXED attains a height of 30cm (12") and bears flowers in shades of crimson, pink, mauve and white. Stocks make good symbiotic partners with ROSES and NICOTIANA SYLVESTRIS.

RAISING ANNUALS FROM SEED:- PART 1 INDOORS

Ideally late April/early May is the best time to be sowing seeds when the days are getting longer and warmer and light levels are increasing with the objective of planting out during early to mid June. Growth during naturally favourable days always produces healthier, stronger plants which quite often will flower as early as six weeks after planting out. Sowing indoors is basically 'intensive care'. Your seeds are not at the mercy of the weather, pests and diseases. It is easy to keep an eye on them and VITAL that you do since their lives are in your hands. Apart from IPOMOEA all the plants I have recommended could hopefully be grown successfully in the open ground (and for some it would be the best bet). 'Hopefully' because there is simply more stacked against them and the survival rate could be less. A cub in a zoo is safer than one in the wild.

Whether you use trays or pots depends on which annuals you are sowing. TRAYS for seeds such as CALENDULA, COSMOS, HOLLYHOCK, LAVATERA and STOCKS. POTS for FOXGLOVE, HORDEUM JUBATUM, and NICOTIANA. Either POTS or the OPEN GROUND for CALIFORNIAN POPPY, CORNFLOWER, GODETIA, GYPSOPHILA, NASTURTIUM, NIGHT SCENTED STOCK and POPPY. OPEN GROUND only for CLARKIA, LARKSPUR, and NIGELLA. You will see from the packets of the seeds chosen for TRAYS that they are less in number than those for POTS; also when you open the packets that the seeds are fairly easily handled and positioned with tweezers. This allows you to place around 50 seeds per tray which will give the resulting seedlings enough room to develop into sturdy little plants; before they can be either transplanted into further trays, individual pots or planted outside after a period of acclimatisation. The seeds for POTS/OPEN GROUND will generally be the size of sand grains. These can be mixed with a little SILVER SAND (available from garden centres) to make it easier to spread evenly from the line in the palm of your hand. Using pots as opposed to open ground will simply give you little clumps of seedlings (the size of cress) which after acclimatisation can be planted in their entirety without root disturbance in specific positions; robust enough to cope with aspects of outdoor life that could have defeated them as emergents in the open ground.

Fill the trays and pots with the seed sowing compost to within 1cm (½") of the top. Level and firm it lightly. Cut a piece of wood to fit into the seed tray and glue a 'handle' on to it to use as a firmer. For pots use a cotton reel with a piece of cane glued into the hole. Stand the trays in water to thoroughly moisten the compost and allow to drain. Sow your seeds. Look on the packet to see if the seeds need to be covered - those which need darkness to germinate will require a light sifting of compost or vermiculite over them while those that need light to get going should just be gently pressed into the compost with your firmer. (Vermiculite creates a humid, warm and aerated micro-climate which lessens the chances of seedlings rotting). Then cover the trays/pots with a sheet of bubble polythene which will retain moisture and also some warmth for night time. Each day give this a shake to release excess moisture and as soon as you see signs of life remove it for good. Make sure that the compost is just moist; neither dry nor wet. Watch trays/pots on sunny windowsills as they can dry out very quickly. On windowsills where sunlight is at a premium place a piece of cardboard covered with aluminium foil behind the trays/pots where the curtains draw to reflect as much light as possible. Do not let the temperature in the room rise and dip dramatically and remember that drawing curtains will drop the temperature on the windowsill. Seedlings will naturally grow towards the strongest light (the window) so to counteract this and keep them straight turn the trays/pots around daily. Seedlings in 'intensive care' are not subjected to movement by wind and rain which actually toughens the stems resulting in sturdy shorter jointed plants. To simulate this brush a sheet of paper over the seedlings for 1½ minutes each day.

Basically seedlings can live in their trays until they have developed two sets of leaves and are easily handled. The best move now is to transplant them into fresh compost (special mix for foxgloves/hollyhocks) either in trays at 3cm (1¼") intervals or individual 9cm (3½") pots. It is possible to plant them in their positions outside after acclimatisation but they really are still a little vulnerable. Growing on will ensure maximum robustness. To transplant the seedlings tease them out of the tray with a little dining fork holding them gently by the LEAVES for the minimum of time. Before doing this wash your hands as the skin's natural oils are not appreciated by young foliage! Firm the seedlings in just slightly deeper than they were in the first tray and lightly water with a fine rose. As your annuals continue to grow some of them such as cosmos will quickly develop a single stem with all their energy going into a dominant bud in an attempt to flower and set seed. There will also be buds where the leaves join the stem. With your thumb and forefinger pinch out the main growing tip just above an opened leaf which will encourage the other buds to develop into shoots. When these have made two sets of leaves you can pinch out the growing tip of these stems. You will then have a robust multi-stemmed plant each stem then being left to produce flower buds. So more flowers to enjoy! The best time to pinch out is early morning when the plant is full of sap.

ANNUALS FROM SEED :- PART 2 OUTDOORS

Your soil has already been prepared for your trees, shrubs, roses, perennials, grasses and bulbs. Annuals generally will appreciate a sunny spot so their leaves can function to capacity but partial shade is quite acceptable. Where you are going to sow use your flathead steel rake to reduce the soil to a crumb-like consistency. Some Blood, Fish and Bone worked in a week or so before sowing will be beneficial. The sun will warm the soil which will now have the necessary air pockets, moisture and nourishment for the plants to succeed. Annuals look more attractive when grown in groups so for the tiny ones mixed with silver sand sprinkle them lightly on the soil which can then be raked very gently before firming with the back of the rake and watering with a fine rose. For the larger seeds rake back a patch of soil to the required depth, water, space the seeds evenly by hand or tweezers and then cover with soil before watering with a fine rose. When the seedlings have developed two sets of leaves they can be thinned out by simply pulling up the surplus or weaker specimens to allow the remainder room for development and pinching out if required.

The seedlings in the trays/pots will need to be acclimatised to the conditions outside before they are planted in their final positions. This is achieved by putting the trays/pots outside in a sheltered position during the day for about 10 days and bringing them inside again late afternoon. Keep them watered if they do not get any rain. Then simply dig holes for them with your trowel planting them slightly deeper than they were in the trays/pots. Take care not to damage them in any way. Keep all your annuals well watered especially during establishment. The FOXGLOVES and HOLLYHOCKS can remain in their pots in a sheltered position until planting them in the border later in the summer for flowering the following summer. Do not forget to take precautions against slugs and snails.

Some of your CORNFLOWERS, COSMOS, CLARKIA, GODETIA and GYPSOPHILA may need to be supported by either neighbouring perennials or bamboo canes/stout twigs. One of the most worthwhile tasks a gardener can perform and it is extremely straightforward is to remove spent flowers from annuals and most perennials. Having been deprived of its instinctive goal of setting seed the plant will return to square one and start to develop new flowers. Also cutting off a faded flower stem will be a likely stimulus for latent buds to develop sideshoots and then more flowering stems. The plants will look cared for and it is enjoyable for a gardener to get amongst the plants at close quarters to check on their wellbeing and become intimate with their beauty and scent.

CHAPTER SIXTEEN
'MAKING THE MOST OF COLOUR'

Colour is at the heart of garden design. Neutral colours such as light/dark browns, greys and greens are the basis being the hues of tree bark, soil and paving. Your house and the hard surfaces in the garden will provide further base colours. Window frames are generally brown or white and there is the colour of the brick or stone work. These are the starting points for the introduction of complimentary and contrasting colours. For example pale/deep pink, yellow and burgundy go well with brown. Beige and green suggest violet-blue, soft rosy-red, lavender, yellow and the many greens of foliage. White invites pastel blue, yellow, pink, silver and white itself. Brick combines with orange, copper, yellow, scarlet, violet-blue, burgundy and peach-pink. A painted rendered wall is a wonderful creative opportunity in that the colour can be chosen to specifically harmonise with your favourite plantings. Equally exciting are the huge range of paint colours which can be custom-mixed by decorating shops. For example a yellow wall would set-off a planting of lavender/purple interspersed with yellow and cream. Blue on the other hand would be a great backdrop for soft orange, golden yellow and copper or conversely lavender, blue, purple, silver and blue-green.

The main colour in a garden is green; the colour of nature herself which acts as a neutral background for the other colours. It is both restful and recessive and enhances other colours through contrast. In fact bold colours look most effective against a background of green. The colour with a wealth of different textures, tones and shades which can alter with the changing light. Glossy dark green will reflect both sun and moon light.

Green effectively highlights the colour white. White is also recessive but acquires luminosity at dusk and in moonlight; reflecting maximum light at all times makes it useful in shady spots. Silver and grey have the same qualities which blend and soften other colours. Silver is especially enhanced by dew and raindrops and the shape, form and texture of silver leaves will be accentuated when seen against a background of dark leaves. The contrast between white and say maroon flowers will be toned down when silver is introduced. Silver makes a wonderful combination with shades of pink (think of ROSES) and blue while grey will add prominence to apricot and light pink. More vibrant colours such as sharp yellow, bronze and purple will work well with silver and grey.

Yellow is the colour of sunshine and easily blends with green. When the sun is lower in the sky from autumn to spring yellow appears at its most radiant. Yellow can be used to diminish shade as it reflects light, as an accent colour and for its luminosity in the warm, fading light of evening. Flowering spires such as FOXGLOVES in creamy-yellow are particularly dramatic at this time. Yellow is a good contrast in the company of blue and purple bringing impact to a planting. Pink and yellow together is improved if purple is brought in since this colour is a mixture of red and blue. Purple like yellow is enhanced when the sun is lower in the sky such as early morning and in the evening. Bright blue appears to intensify the brightness of yellow giving it a golden aura. Creamy-yellow can be used to soften the impact of other colours. Yellow, white and grey adds vibrance to a planting in sunlight. Orange; another dominant colour combines well with soft amber, white, yellow, pinks and purple. Maroon too is a good choice with yellow, silver, blue and white.

Blue is an interesting colour; relaxing and recessive in paler hues while the brighter shades can be quite dominant. Light blue is particularly effective in shade. Blues appear at their absolute best in the spring when leaf colour is at its most vibrant and providing the best contrast. Bringing purple and blue together seems to enrich the blue especially in sunlight. Pink combines well with blue especially pinky-blue, also mauve, pale cream and blush colours. All pastel colours bring lightness and airiness to plantings and their prominence lasts into the gloaming. With these colours in the picture white will appear quite ethereal.

Red is the most dominant colour contrasting harshly with green which is a problem that can be eased by bringing in purple and yellow which adds a complimentary richness. Red and purple are at their best in sun (fading into obscurity with the dusk). A good illustration of the two colours together is the dark purple foliage and red flowers of DAHLIA BISHOP OF LLANDAFF. Orange and purple is a striking contrast as well. In small spaces darker colours tend to bring a calming influence to bright reds, oranges and yellows.

The performance of all colours is determined by the fluid movement of light. As the sun spends the days going round your garden from east to west its intensity is ever changing. Shadows coming and going; creating an aura which unfolds minute by minute through every day of every season. We have seen how twilight intensifies some colours and diminishes others, slanting late afternoon sunlight will heighten the contrast between light and dark colours. Lengthening shadows will appear to give the garden more depth especially when the sun is low in the sky. Shafts of sunlight not only illuminate but change the intensity of colour as can the sky itself. If clouds are scudding light will intensify and fade rapidly with shadows rolling in and out. A leaden sky will create the same effect as dusk. Sunlight after rain will see raindrops become coloured jewels. And trees and flowers will cast their shadows on other plants creating enchanting, flickering miniature patterns of light playing on colour. Morning mist especially in summer diffuses sunlight so colour is seen as through a veil.

To create the illusion of a longer garden place dominant reds and oranges near the house and recessive blues, lilacs and silvers for example in the distance. Obviously the reverse will make the garden appear shorter. Bi-colours are best seen at close quarters and single colours from afar.

CHAPTER SEVENTEEN
'ARTISTIC INTERLUDES AROUND THE GARDEN'

Although plants are pivotal in a garden their influence can be enhanced by the inclusion of statues, sculpture, pots, urns and other ornamental accessories. Used in moderation and with feeling they can unite all the other components of the garden creating a unique ambience. They will also provide structural interest throughout the year. All need to be in scale with the garden as a whole.

STATUES are time-honoured features with attitudes that bring animation into the garden which can be effectively employed. For example a statue's gaze can be focussed on a pleasant tree, planting or view. Its prescence could enliven a shady corner or compliment or contrast a particular tree or shrub. A statue needs to be placed with careful consideration; basically larger figures are more effective at a distance and smaller ones at closer range. It should stand comfortably as part of your planting yet have its own space in which to make its mark (ideally where birds do not make theirs!). Statues are usually in neutral colours which integrate well with those of the surrounding plants. In time a statue in a sunny position will acquire a patina of crusty lichens while another in the shade will become mossy. Both conducive to natural harmony. Statues that are time-worn have the most character; perhaps with some history attached which will command a high price. And sadly a hefty insurance premium and the worry of security. However some damaged figures can be appealing and not too expensive. Recently made pieces with respect for past times can be mellowed by brushing on some natural yoghurt after placement. This will help to kick-start the growth of lichens or moss. Statues can be attractively 'framed' by an encirclement of GRASSES for the breeze and light to play with. In low sunlight a statue will cast a dramatic long shadow. Including a piece of work by a promising artist will bring individuality to the garden and encouragement to its creator.

Ceramic, earthenware, stone and terracotta POTS/URNS have all been created from materials that the earth itself has yielded. So they are naturally at one with the house and composition of the garden; their shapes, textures and neutral hues the perfect foil for plant associations. Practically they need to be frostproof. They are focal points in their own right and allow plants to feature in places without soil such as paved areas or on inspection covers. They also provide a home for plants with special needs such as a particular growing medium. The plants should not obscure the attraction of the pot/urn which should have good drainage holes and small stones in the bottom to keep them free. If you can find pots bearing a local potter's name, perhaps from the past then this will provide further interest. Use John Innes potting compost No 2 or 3.

Ideal for pots and urns are FERNS - real focal points with their diversity of fronds in an assortment of shapes, textures, colours and sizes. Ferns in pots will need to be kept well watered and should be in shady areas. Add some bark chippings (from garden centres) to the compost when potting ferns to help create the cool, moisture retentive well-drained soil of woodland. An occasional feed with a seaweed based fertiliser at 1 tablespoon per 2 gallon watering can will be appreciated. They can remain undisturbed for a number of years and just need the old fronds removing in spring after they have protected the crowns over the winter. Be careful not to damage the crowns and emerging fronds which will unfurl so elegantly during late spring. If there are some red TULIPS or red-barked CORNUS ALBA SIBIRICA in the picture the new pale green fronds will be even more dramatic. Later pink ASTILBE and the Madonna and Regal LILIES would look effective with the developed fronds. CAMPANULA PERSICIFOLIA ALBA would be an ideal companion for ferns showing up well in the shade and giving effective contrast with the fern's tracery. So too would ASTRANTIA and ANEMONE BLANDA WHITE SPLENDOUR. Fronds caught in shafts of sunlight are particularly striking.

It is also worth including some ferns in an area of the border which remains moist in summer and has shade for at least part of the day. The ground below trees and shrubs is a possibility especially if you have planted some HELLEBORES, HOSTAS (especially green and white ones), and PRIMROSES which will be complimentary. If you can lay your hands on a few pieces of attractive fallen timber or logs then place these around the ferns to provide a natural backdrop (especially if they become mossy). After planting you could get some pine bark chippings to spread around for added effect and to retain moisture. In spring when you remove the old fronds put some chippings up to where the fronds were attached and water with some seaweed fertiliser. Ferns are available from hardy plant nurseries and garden centres. Varieties of ATHYRIUM, DRYOPTERIS, POLYSTICHUM, MATTEUCCIA, POLYPODIUM and ONOCLEA are recommended.

GRASSES make ideal subjects for pots and urns as striking vertical

accents and attractive cascades. Especially those with fountain-like or arching forms. Recommended are :-
STIPA TENUISSIMA, STIPA ARUNDINACEA, PENNISETUM ALOPECUROIDES HAMELN, MILIUM EFFUSUM AUREA, CAREX COMANS BRONZE (especially in a salt-glazed pot/urn), FESTUCA GLAUCA ELIJAH BLUE and HAKONECHLOA MACRA AUREOLA.

In Chapter Five it was suggested that gaps be left between the components of the paving so that plants could be incorporated. The flowers of HERBS not only blur the boundaries between path and border but the heat from the stone, brick or concrete will cause the essential oils to be warmed and released more freely. So stronger fragrance when the plants are brushed or even walked on. THYMES are ideal plants for this feature forming thick evergreen mats resilient enough to withstand a footprint or two and having attractive colour, texture and scent. A mecca for bees too! Thymes enjoy the sunshine but appreciate good drainage so some horticultural grit would be worthwhile in the planting gaps along with some organic matter for nourishment. The wild thyme THYMUS SERPYLLUM has purple-red flowers in late summer. T. x CITRIODORUS the lemon-scented thyme has pale green leaves and pink flowers. CHAMOMILE is also a suitable plant especially CHAMAEMELUM NOBILE TRENEAGUE which roots easily in gaps and has strongly scented foliage. MENTHA PULEGIUM the PENNYROYAL MINT has tubular lilac flowers and aromatic bright green leaves thriving especially in moisture retentive positions. M. REQUIENII the mat-forming shade loving CORSICAN MINT has similar flowers and bright green peppermint-scented leaves. Thymes and mints should be cut back after flowering to maintain vigour and compactness, chamomile more regularly. VIOLA TRICOLOR - Heartsease or the Wild Pansy does well in gaps bearing flowers in shades of purple, lavender, white or yellow. The upper petals are often dark purple while the lower ones just have dark purple streaks. Evergreen and flowers from spring to autumn. A prolific self-seeder which will do best in more shady moisture retentive areas. Which will also suit VINCA MINOR the LESSER PERIWINKLE which is mat-forming and evergreen with dark green leaves bearing depending on variety violet, pale blue, reddish-purple or white flowers. Cut back in early spring to keep in check.

Cracks in paving are handy places for seeds from the rest of the garden to colonise. and this makes for a natural random effect. It pays not to be too enthusiastic about weeding cracks until you know for sure what is coming up! Any plant which settles itself tends to thrive even in conditions that gardeners would never have tried them in! Gaps can be filled with seed sowing compost in an attempt to encourage an interesting medley of self-sets or to sow a mixture of your choice. Always remember to water these plants at the start but go easy on watering to encourage roots to strike out for moisture. Also not to stuff big rootballs into small gaps!

There should always be room for at least one SEAT in a garden. A favourite place simply to enjoy what you have created. A seat is always better with a surrounding such as a planting, fence, wall or hedge to give it cosiness. A sunny area is the most pleasant especially when evening sun leaves its warmth in wood, brick, stone and concrete long after it has slid below the horizon. Scent such as LAVENDER is significant and is accentuated in the evening (and after rain) along with the sound of a zephyr passing through leaves. In fading light ROSES, LILIES and HONEYSUCKLES appear to almost be lit from within such is their luminosity. Leave fallen rose petals for another dimension. The colour of a wooden or metal seat is worth considering as this can itself add value to the surrounding planting. It could be in an accent colour to link the seat with the house and also the planting. Neutral colours such as pale grey, grey/blue and green are favourites. You may even start dreaming of a gazebo or summerhouse! Trees and shrubs can in time be pruned so the natural sculpture of their trunks and branches is revealed while opening up views through them to other parts of the garden.

Recycling although a buzz-word of today has always been at the heart of gardening. Through IMAGINATION redundant articles are seen as accessories which will add uniqueness to a garden. For example a potential planter is ANYTHING that in your opinion has shape, form and texture, so long as it has drainage or can be drilled for drainage with the ability to hold moisture for as long as a traditional plant pot. A basket lined with a thick piece of polythene and brushed with three coats of yacht varnish becomes a complimentary plant home. Reclaimed chimney pots have beautiful shapes and their terracotta and salt-glazed forms blend with pots, urns and plants. Even old broken clay flowerpots can add sculptural charm. Rusty metal melds well with yellows, pinks, oranges, lilacs and silvers. As the elements return the metal to the ground from which the ore to make it came it all seems in keeping with the natural cycle of the garden itself. If you do not want rust RED OXIDE paint will weather to a terracotta shade and texture. “There is no such thing as art; only artists” said Ernest Gombrich the great art historian. So keep your eyes open imaginatively; a piece of junk could become a jewel in your garden.

Garden tools past their digging days can make attractive plant supports in the border while old watering cans around lend more shape and form either as working tools or as planters/ornaments. An old wheelbarrow continues this nostalgic thread which runs through most gardens containing as they do so many plants, ideas and materials from the past.

CHAPTER EIGHTEEN
'A POT-POURRI OF TIPS AND ENCOURAGEMENT'

So now you have a garden. A harmonious planting of trees, shrubs, roses, perennials, grasses, spring bulbs and annuals. Every one an individual star but through your design their combined qualities choreographed into seasonal acts for a 365 day performance. You should be justly proud of what you have created and be excited at its prospects. Everything has been done that could have been done and its odds-on that your preparation, planning and planting will reward you. Success is ultimately down to nurture and Nature in partnership. Which just occasionally may feel like the skilful against the wilful!

As a gardener your brief is to keep all your plants happy. You have learnt how deadheading and pruning will utilise a plant's natural inclinations to give the best display. And how keeping the garden free of weeds and debris relieves plants of competition and lessens the chances of pests and disease. These jobs all mean that you get amongst your plants regularly which is good for several reasons. You can admire the plants which is why you got them in the first place - their character, scent and colour. Spot pests and diseases in the early stages with time to take action. Look if there are any self-sets. See if any plants need to be divided. Note schemes that are not really hitting the spot for you and what could be done to rectify them. Rejoice when things do what you had in mind for them and be pleasantly surprised when you discover wonderful plant associations that have happened by accident! Wonder at the growth of plants from the first shoots through to bud, flower and seedhead. Especially when buds are perhaps minutes away from opening. Start weeding before growth really starts; be careful where you tread and keep on top of this job throughout the year remembering every weed pulled up or scuffled is one less able to reproduce.

As your garden matures and develops so will your experience which will tell you instinctively what needs to be done and when to keep everything looking good. You will find gardening is an enjoyable rolling programme of jobs. Whatever you do you can stand back and SEE what you have achieved and KNOW that you have made a contribution to your garden's long-term development and character. Because a garden constantly evolves it is never completed. But work is rarely boring simply because it varies through the seasons; you are fine tuning your own creation as the weather springs transient magical moments all around.

Of course the weather can just as easily turn nasty and your garden will suffer just as it can at the mercy of pests and diseases. A local farmer once remarked "the problem with livestock is that they can easily become deadstock" - the same can happen to plants; even those seemingly given the best of everything. Age can certainly weary and condemn them. But you will be able to work around this. As your experience grows so will your alertness; grubbing out casualties and replanting becomes just another part of the rolling programme causing minimum disruption to the overall impact of your garden. Every good garden is as it is today because of continual adjustment, refining and reworking over time by gardeners; constantly gaining experience and CONFIDENCE to try out new ideas. Some of which will work and some will not but accomplished gardeners are always those who dared to put their ideas into practice.

Weeding and tidying beneficial as it is removes a potential source of organic matter from entering the soil's ecosystem. Many gardeners create 'compost heaps' from the accumulations of garden 'waste' which over time and with much diligence from the gardener produces fine organic matter to return to the soil. There are several container systems available to take the place of heaps. However all take up space and are unattractive especially in the smaller garden. As most local authorities provide households with wheelie bins for green waste it seems easier to simply make use of this facility along with recycling centres. The waste is fast-tracked into compost by heating to a temperature sufficient to kill seeds, pests and disease. It is sold quite cheaply and makes a quality mulch. If you can hide a few binliners fill them up with damp fallen leaves, puncture and leave for a year when the 'leaf mould' can be crumbled through your hands and spread on the soil. A long-term commitment to seasonally adding by mulch organic matter such as manure, compost and leaf mould will ensure that there is a constant supply of plant food stored in the soil. In a way doing manually what nature would do automatically. In time mulching is likely to alter the acidity/alkalinity of the soil and if this is of interest further soil tests as explained in Chapter 2 are recommended at intervals.

In severe cases of pests/disease where chemical control is the last resort use only organic pesticides which are derived from plants and break down into harmless compounds. But if you are watchful this situation is unlikely to arise and many pests such as aphids and small caterpillars in moderation are simply dinner for young birds such as tits.

Your grass will require cutting once a week during the growing season with the mower blades gradually lowered from the initial cuts of new sward to give a cut height of 3cm (1½") each cut. This will encourage smooth dense growth. An even cut is achieved by starting mowing in a different position and alternating from a north/south direction to east/west each mowing. In times of drought cutting will be required less often with the blades set slightly higher. Never fret over brown grass it always greens up quickly when the rain comes! Watering simply is a waste of water and impractical. A sprinkler would take ages to give grass the water it would get from natural rainfall. And it would not be operating in the same conditions so would continually be fighting evaporation. The grass roots instead of going down further to seek moisture would take the easier option of aiming for that which had just managed to penetrate the surface. Leaving them in fact more vulnerable to drought by being nearer the sun's rays. The best thing is to give rainfall an easy passage to the root run. Push your garden fork into the grass ideally at 25cm (10") intervals to a depth of 9cm (3½") some time in autumn; pressing down and pulling back slightly to create channels through which water and air can permeate. Spring too if you can face it! Grass in good condition is less susceptible to weed invasion. Certain weeds such as clover which provides nectar for bees in my opinion are acceptable but as with your borders spotting weeds and dealing with them straight away will mean a less problematic future.

ANNEX: 'TOOL UP'

Over time the top growth of grass becomes clogged by dead grass, leaves, moss and fragments of vegetation from the garden. This excludes light and air making it difficult for the grass to produce new shoots. This can all be removed with a SPRINGBOK RAKE which has springy steel tines arranged in a gentle arc radiating from a central steel frame. When pulled towards you it has the necessary power to remove all the offending 'thatch'. A 'SCARIFIER RAKE' manufactured by Wolf Garden Ltd. has sharp steel tines on a wheeled axle which penetrate deeply giving a particularly thorough comb with less muscular effort than the springbok. A TAPROOT WEEDER is essential for removing unsightly deep-rooted and rosette-forming weeds from your grass which should be done before they flower and seed. Basically this is two prongs at the end of a longish angled steel shaft with a handle. This allows the tool to be inserted deeply alongside the taproot which can then be carefully prised from the ground.

In time the grass may need the odd repair. Worn patches can be pricked with a fork around September to a depth of 5cm (2") to loosen the soil before sowing some seed. Cover with a light sprinkling of John Innes compost and keep moist during establishment. Bumps and hollows can be rectified simply by cutting the turf with your half-moon edger and rolling it back either adding some soil or taking it away before replacing the turf. Brush some John Innes into the cracks.

In mid-spring you can apply some Blood, Fish and Bone or seaweed based feed on to the grass at the rate of a good handful per square metre/yard. Spent mushroom compost brushed in would be an alternative.

Until your shrubs and trees mature beyond a thickness of 25mm (1") pruning can be done with your hand pruners. Beyond that you will need a couple of further tools:-

ANNEX: 'TOOL UP'

Firstly some LOPPERS which are long-handled pruners capable of cutting through branches up to whatever diameter is given on the packaging. The long handles allow you to exert a huge leverage while giving you a greater reach into the plant. Models with telescopic handles increase this capability. Ideally choose on specification - curved deep-forged precision ground blades which keep sharper for longer and rubber shock-absorbing grips on the handles. Make sure the loppers feel 'just right' in your hands. Secondly a PRUNING SAW which tackles branches beyond the scope of loppers (but below those for your BOW SAW). Teeth which cut on both the push and pull strokes are the most efficient. Also longer blades with fewer but deeper cut teeth get through thicker branches more quickly. More teeth on shorter blades make finer cuts on smaller branches. Hardened, tempered steel blades are recommended. A curved blade will give easier access in awkward or confined spaces. Again the saw should feel comfortable in your hands.

Basically pruning is the removal of unwanted growth due to weakness, disease or death. It may be getting in your way, impeding the growth of other plants or detrimental to the plant's own development e.g. crossing branches. Weak, diseased or dead wood needs to be cut back to healthy wood. Obstructive branches MUST be pruned to a healthy bud which will develop into a new branch. This should be pointing in a direction which will not obviously cause future hindrance. If the tree has two opposite buds you can rub out the one that is not required. Large branches should be taken back to the edge of the thickened ring just before the branch joins the trunk. It is vital always to make clean tidy cuts to minimise the risk of disease and to encourage the tree to produce healing tissue. A weighty branch requires a three-way cut. About 30cm (12") from the final cut saw upwards from the underneath ⅓ through the branch. Then 5cm (2") from this cut going away from the trunk make a second cut until the major part of the branch comes away up to the undercut. The final cut can then be made in line with the thickened ring from top to bottom. Use your grafting knife to smooth any rough edges to the cut.

Knowing both your own and your tools capabilities is important when pruning. Large branches which require ladders to reach are best tackled by QUALIFIED INSURED arboriculturalists who are worth your money when your well-being (and your tree's) are at stake. Also if you are unsure of the best course of action do not risk maiming your tree for life; get an expert opinion. Basically if the tool you are trying to use is struggling then you need the next one in your armoury. 1) Hand pruners. 2) Loppers. 3) Pruning saw. With hand pruners holding them thin blade downwards brings that cutting blade nearer the trunk enabling a cut to be made flush with the trunk without leaving a stump which could be an entry for disease. The thin blade should always be nearest to the bud when pruning. It is best to prune in winter when trees are dormant so you can literally 'see the wood for the trees' - i.e. the complete structural picture. Take care not to damage yourself or other plants when pruning larger branches.

In tune with the natural organic approach to gardening is leaving a few dried-out stems and seed heads to stand the winter. As well as highlighting the structure of trees and shrubs winter light, dew and frost can also dramatise the skeletons of summer which will also have a delightful movement and rattle in the breeze. Spiders attach their webs which become ethereal jewellery with frost and dew while birds find seeds to eat and insects such as ladybirds shelter. Particularly good are ALLIUM, ECHINACEA, FOENICULUM VULGARE PURPUREUM, SEDUM and ERYNGIUM.

Do involve children in your gardening if you can. There is no better way of learning about life and respect for all living things. My interest in gardening undoubtedly stems from when as a four year-old I was taken by my mother to buy some seeds of annuals. The subsequent sowing and growing was a wonderful introduction to a life cycle. As well as being aesthetically and sensorily stimulating. Watching THEIR seeds come into life and assisting in raising them to flowering plants instills in a child a creative disposition. As well as basic organisation and method skills (importantly sometimes learning from failure due to mistakes or influences beyond their control). Conversely working with plants and gardens has proved successful in reversing the destructive inclinations of lawbreakers.

The Latin names of plants appear at first sight somewhat intimidating. But really they are very explicit. Basically the first part of the name refers to the genus which is simply a group of plants with similar characteristics. The second part refers to species which is a sub-group of one or more plants with similar characteristics within the genus. These reflect facts about the plant such as the region, country or continent of origin. Or habitat say woodland, mountain or near water (all indicative of the type of conditions it requires). Also it may give a clue to the plant's appearance such as size, habit, flower, fruit, leaf or colour. Perhaps a commemoration for the person who found or raised the plant or for a relative or acquaintance of theirs.

The following are often encountered:-

COUNTRIES -
ARABIS=ARABIA,
JAPONICA=JAPAN,
ORIENTALIS=ORIENT,
CHINENSIS=CHINA,
OCCIDENTALIS=AMERICA,
SIBIRICA=SIBERIA.

COLOURS -
ALBA=WHITE,
CARDINALIS–RED,
NIGRA=BLACK,
AUREUS=GOLD,
PURPUREA=PURPLE.

HABITAT -
ALPINUS=ALPINE,

MONTANA=MOUNTAIN,
SYLVATICA=FOREST,
CAMPESTRIS=FIELD,
PRATENSIS=MEADOW.

GROWTH HABIT -
COLUMNARIS=COLUMNAR,
DENTATA=TOOTHED,
LANATA=WOOLLY,
COMPRESSA=CLOSELY PACKED,
FRUTICOSA=BUSHY,
REPENS=CREEPING.

Others you will come across are:-
FOLIA=FOLIAGE, FLORA=FLOWER,
FLORIBUNDA=CLUSTER FLOWERING,
GRANDIFLORA=LARGE FLOWERS,
ANGUSTIFOLIA=NARROW LEAVES,
CORDATA/CORDIFOLIA=HEART SHAPED,
HEPATICA=LIVER COLOURED/SHAPED,
LATIFOLIA=BROAD LEAVED,
MACROPHYLLA=LARGE LEAVED,
MICROPHYLLA=SMALL LEAVED,
PALMATA=HAND SHAPED,
PETIOLARE=LONG STALKED,
ROTUNDIFOLIA=ROUND,
SERRATA=SAW EDGED.